FROM LIGHT TO SOUND

THE SPIRITUAL PROGRESSION

DENNIS HOLTJE

PUBLISHED BY MASTERPATH, INC.
(NON-PROFIT)

www.masterpath.org

Published by MasterPath, Inc., (a non-profit corporation)
P.O. Box 9035, Temecula, CA, 92589 U.S.A.

Printed in the United States of America

First Printing, Nov. 1995   5000 copies
Second Printing, June 1996   5000 copies
Third Printing, October 1997   5000 copies
Fourth Printing, December 2000   5000 copies

Publisher's Cataloging in Publication Data

Holtje, Dennis R.
    From Light to Sound: the spiritual progression / Dennis Holtje —
Albuquerque, N.M. : MasterPath, Inc., 1995.
      p.   cm.
    Includes bibliographic references and index.
    ISBN 1–885949-00-6

    1. Soul. 2. Consciousness—Religious aspects. I. Title.

BL290.H56 1995   299'.93
                                    QBI95-20338

Cover art by Ana Maria Mastrogiovanni.

ON THE COVER

The swan is an ancient symbol of ultimate spiritual purity. It is shown here ascending beyond the rocky shoals of its earthbound existence into the state of original purity from whence it came. This flight symbolizes the inner journey of soul's unfoldment through the many layers of consciousness within our own being.

PREFACE

There once was a beautiful white swan that came from the great ocean to the North. After being in the South for the winter, it was ready for the return journey home. So it took off and with its big wing span and shining white feathers, it soared effortlessly through the blue sky. After a long while, and far along the journey, the swan began to tire and came down to land for a rest. It landed right on the edge of a water well and let out a deep sigh.

In the bottom of this well there lived a frog. The frog said, "Well, who are you and where do you come from?"

"I am a swan, and my home is on the water of the great northern ocean," answered the swan.

"Ocean? How big is this ocean?" asked the frog.

"Very big," said Swan.

"Is it this big?" Frog asked, taking two hops backward.

"No, much bigger," said Swan.

So the frog took five huge hops backward, saying, "Is the ocean this big?"

Swan said, "No, it's much bigger than that."

And so the frog went around the entire well—his whole reality, as he knew it—and asked the swan, "Now, is the ocean as big as this?" And the swan said, "No, it's much, much bigger!"

Thereupon the frog said, "Well, you're a fool and a liar!" because he knew there could be nothing bigger than his world and his well.

TABLE OF CONTENTS

LIST OF ILLUSTRATIONS

INTRODUCTION

The greatest desire of spiritual seekers is to fulfill their spiritual dream! We all are innately aware that a deeper truth exists within us than our day-to-day existence and mundane concerns would indicate. Our dream is to discover and live life from this more encompassing state of being. We long for freedom from our limitations, from the layers of learned behavior, borrowed thought, and temporary appeasements that limit our experience and expression in life. These limitations often produce the haunting feeling of being a prisoner of an identity that we do not wholly enjoy, yet we appear to be fused to it, and to perpetuate it.

Our fondest and most heartfelt dreams would allow us to free ourselves from such entrapment. The purpose of the spiritual life is to enable the seeker to make these dreams come true. To realize the freedom which is our spiritual inheritance and birthright, we must first come to know the contents of our "well," and then be brave and bold enough to venture beyond its confining walls. In the beginning of our journey, our faith alone allows us to enter into the spiritual life. Faith by itself does not provide the necessary sustaining power to bring us to our spiritual goal, just as merely dreaming about owning a new car is a far cry from the effort and saving it takes to acquire one. Eventually, greater levels of making spiritual truth both real and tangible need to be sought and made our own. This spiritual quest motivates truth seekers to continue their search after they have drawn all they can from their current religions, metaphysical paths, or solitary quests for deeper meaning to life. This yearning for greater, deeper, more intimate contact with soul and the God within, based on our personal experiences, can lead us past the restrictions of religious dogma and the uncertainty of metaphysics to the next stage of our spiritual unfoldment.

The point comes in the life of every sincere spiritual seeker when information, knowledge, and finespun theory no longer satisfy our innate quest for spiritual liberation. Paths based on the upliftment received from greater knowledge, information, and metaphysical imagery—intriguing and valuable as they may be—are products of the spiritual current known as "the light." Should we desire a more fulfilling spiritual relationship with soul and the God within, we must surpass the reach of this light energy and experience the spiritual energy which parents it—the Sound Current. There is a spiritual progression from light to Sound—when the light has served its purpose, the Sound appears.

Just what is the spiritual energy known as Sound? What are the distinctions between these two spiritual forces of light and Sound, and why can this progression be so vitally important to the seeker? We will explore the answers to these questions within this book's pages. Hopefully, what is written here will also help clarify differences between the many modes of spiritual thinking, including religion and the psychic arts, and their potential benefits and limitations, as we explore how these practices compare with the system of enlightenment known as the Light and Sound teachings.

Humankind's spiritual endeavor is to establish and fully mature its innate identity as soul. The catalyst for such lofty spiritual attainments is the Light and Sound energies that exist within our own bodies. The ancient teachings of Light and Sound have developed over millennia of study and experience with these great spiritual energies. They still provide a contemporary statement of many great adepts' explorations of the Creator's universal design, Its divine laws and principles, and the purpose of humankind in creation. These precepts help spiritual seekers better understand our own divine nature, thereby giving us a means to create and enliven a purer, truer identification with the stunning beauty of soul—our own true self and hidden identity.

No particular group or denomination can claim a monopoly on these teachings; therefore this book is written from a viewpoint which does not endorse nor contest any specific spiritual group or path. Principles and tenets of this system underlie nearly every major religion, philosophy, metaphysical study, and native system of spiritual practice within the world. Throughout history, great masters, teachers, and saints have taught these principles of Light and Sound. However, spiritual truth is so far removed from what the masses conceive it to be that they often rise up to slay its purest vessels. Therefore, these precepts have usually been couched in religious rhetoric, given in diluted form, or taught through parable and metaphor to avoid offending kings, emperors, and religious establishments.

Fortunately, the general level of public tolerance regarding spirituality on our planet has risen to a point where the divine principles can now be presented in a far more open and direct way to a spiritually thirsty public. The works of great masters such as Jesus, Buddha, Kabir, Rumi, Shamas-i-Tabriz, Sawan Singh Ji, and many more have led to the creation of a spiritual environment within which the Light and Sound can now openly flourish.

Many souls are looking for an explanation to bridge the gap between where their search has led, and where they wish to arrive. This book has been written to offer insights for these seekers and for all who desire to experience deeper spiritual meaning in their lives. It has been written in love for all sincere seekers of truth who, unlike the frog, question the diameter and depth of their own wells; who have the courage to recognize their own needs for increased wisdom and clarity; and who are open-minded enough to listen, contemplate, experiment, and learn.

No miracle is greater and no truth more sublime than the miracle of growth. The attributes of love and understanding are twin traits of the Divine which penetrate each other. When our understanding is broadened one iota, then so too is our love for soul and for God, and this book will be an unqualified success.

Dennis Holtje
Santa Fe, New Mexico
July 1995

THE JOURNEY OF

SOUL'S UNFOLDMENT

Chapter 1

Knowing Ourselves as Soul

We are all spiritual beings seeking to rediscover our true nature—that hidden, spiritual part in each of us that we call soul. Soul is the all-powerful and all-present part of our being that never dies. It is our primary and most basic unit of awareness; it knows no boundaries of time or space. Through this divine faculty we communicate with God, and the splendor of the Creator's essence is revealed to us.

In their own spiritual journeys to realization of self and God, the Masters of Light and Sound have endured great pain and suffering; but true happiness, wisdom, and joy have been their rewards. Such a journey to truth and beauty brings with it the price of great pain and suffering because in order to reach the depths of our own being, we have much work to do and many false gods to leave behind.

Before we can experience the fullness of our spiritual inheritance, we must first understand soul's plight.

Finding Soul Within

> *Within this house is everything.*
> *Nothing is without.*
> *Those who seek outside are in delusion.*

Guru Nanak
16th century Sikh guru and
Master of Light and Sound

As human beings, we are indeed complex; our makeup is more varied and subtle than we can imagine. The physical body certainly has many needs and desires of its own, just as do the mental, the emotional, and the subconscious selves. Looking further, we may wonder about soul's need to express its inherent beauty and divinity. In our culture we hear constant references to soul and its qualities; but if you ask almost anyone to define soul, you might be surprised how unsure we all can be as to just what soul is. Soul and God are identical in their qualities or traits.

Some of the great teachers have pointed out that soul is the drop of water and God is the ocean—and that although the drop and the ocean are different, their essence and composition are the same. Soul is impregnated with love, wisdom, and power; it is changeless, timeless, and beyond our ability to fathom with the mind. Thus we find soul so difficult to define, yet we feel that we can relate to the concept of soul even if we can't define it. This dilemma leads us to the situation which all humanity faces.

Great writers have used the analogy of the battlefield to describe humanity's spiritual plight. Each part of our being is like an army trying to dominate the battlefield of our consciousness. The prize is not status, territory, or wealth, but the attention of the individual and which of our many component parts will dominate our attention for its own fulfillment. In this call to battle, how loud is the battle cry of soul?

It is fairly simple to define our physical needs for food, water, sleep, elimination, warmth, etc. Our emotional needs can be somewhat more difficult—we want love, acceptance, happiness, someone to talk to, someone to listen; we want to feel good. Yet what we must give to satisfy these needs often clouds the issue. Our mental desires are even more nebulous. We want to think clearly and act rationally, yet so many issues have large gray areas that don't break down into black and white, and we also have to deal with our emotions and subconscious desires, even as we attempt to think clearly.

Often, by the time we begin to hear the small, subtle voice of soul within us, the battle has already been lost. We have expended our energies in satisfying our physical, emotional, and mental needs and desires. The voice of soul, which is of the essence of God as well as our way of staying in touch with the Divine, is silenced or extremely muted. This is the spiritual dilemma within each of us.

Thus, soul, our highest faculty and most basic unit of awareness, is trapped—a prisoner in its own home. Its position of supremacy within our constitution has been usurped by our conditioned thinking, our mechanical emotional responses, and our rampant desires which overcome soul by dominating our attention. This entrapment of soul is why we can talk about it, allude to it, and philosophize about it, but we can't quite identify with it or even define it. Isn't it wonderful, however, to know that a faculty above the mind even exists, difficult as it may be to define?

This condition must be reversed for liberation to be won. However, it requires great personal effort on the part of the sincere seeker to change the outcome of the battle. The mind, ego, emotions, and habitual patterns of behavior will not roll over and play dead at the first sign of challenge; but with strong, persistent, personal effort, and the love and guidance of a true spiritual Master, the battle is an assured victory.

It is never our state of grace that separates us from God—only our state of mind, for we are all essentially and innately spiritual beings, and soul is our true identity. But until we make the inner journey through the layers of mind and emotions that separate ourselves from soul, our true identity remains hidden. This spiritual sojourn is really a journey of remembering our true self.

Soul remains after the physical body is put to rest and the concerns of mind and emotion cease. The religious idea of salvation generally states that we do not meet our higher self until after the demise of the body. But if we cannot contact soul while still living within the body, can we be so sure that death will provide us with this opportunity?

Sincere seekers of truth can get answers to these questions of the ages. The answers will never come through speculation, faith, or philosophy; only the inner spiritual journey of self-remembrance can provide them. As spiritual seekers, our true purpose in life is none other than self-discovery. How long will we endure the ego and all its concerns to continue to rule the roost? How long are we willing to live in confusion, seeking pleasures and fleeing from pain? How long will the cocoon remain intact, stifling the beautiful butterfly within? These are the questions that face us as we set our feet upon the road to self-discovery.

Living life is the experience through which we may come to know ourselves as soul. As we grow and unfold in spiritual wisdom and maturity, the question of life's purpose takes on new meaning. Merely living to fulfill our physical, mental, and emotional needs becomes less and less important to us, and pride, honor, community standing, and prestige no longer fulfill us as they once did. As soul, we live in the physical world to experience life; and life, with all its joys and sufferings, is our teacher. The world provides the perfect stage for the experiences we need to discover our true selves. So the answer to the question, "How long are we willing to live under the predominating influences of mind, emotion, and ego?" is directly related to our experience as soul.

When our desire to experience more of our true selves becomes greater than our lower desires' tendencies to satiate the mind and ego, then we become willing to walk into the light. Our experiences in many incarnations and in many bodies are like streams that feed into one mighty river. All lead inexorably to the great experience of meeting soul, our true self.

This understanding of our true nature and the ability to express it takes time. Before we can know our true selves, many false gods or false identities must be exposed to the light of truth. Reality is approached through illusion, so we go through many lifetimes and life forms to learn who we are not, before we come to see ourselves as soul. Consider the multitude of identities the mind and emotions can create: male, female, good husband or wife, mother, rich man, patriot, loser, etc. The list is almost endless. There is nothing wrong with possessing the qualities of any of the above identities, when we choose to do so. However, when we form binding emotional and mental ties to such qualities, we tend to identify with them to such a degree that we become the lesser identity; and our true nature as soul loses the ability to express itself. It is on life's stage that this divine drama has the chance to unfold!

After many, many lifetimes, when soul's desire comes to the fore, the average person becomes the seeker. All identities of the mind and the emotions lose their appeal, and we have an innate desire to unfold as spiritual beings. This desire comes from soul, not from the mind or the emotions. The seeker no longer runs about in the world trying to satiate desires through worldly comforts and pleasures. We know that soul lies within, and only by learning how to come into greater and greater contact with its love, wisdom, freedom, and power will we ever be truly happy.

What is Light and What is Sound?

High above in the Lord's mansion
*   ringeth the transcendental music.*
But, alas, the unlucky hear Him not;
They are in deep slumber.

> Guru Nanak
> 16th century Sikh guru and
> Master of Light and Sound

Sound, stars, and light are all inside.

> Maharaj Sardar Bahadur Jagat Singh
> 20th century Master of Light and Sound

The Universe was manifested out of
*   the Divine Sound;*
From It came into being the Light.

> Shamas-i-Tabriz
> 13th century Persian saint and
> Master of Light and Sound

Many great teachers, masters, and avatars have referred to the Current of Consciousness which emanates from the Godhead. This all-sustaining and pervasive current makes all life possible. It is responsible for all creation as well as all destruction; no rose can bloom nor rain fall without Its life-sustaining impulses.

This all-nourishing Light and Sound has been called by many names throughout the world. The Christian faith generally refers to it as the *Word of God*. In India it is known as the *Nam*. The Greeks refer to it as the *Logos,* and the Sufis call it the *Vadan*. Within the Light and Sound teachings, it is often referred to as the *Sound Current* or the *Audible Life Stream*. This divine current is the breath of life of all God's creation, and all creation is the universal body of God. This Sound Current, or Holy Spirit, is composed of two basic elements: Light and Sound. The great river of spirit constantly flows around and through each of us and can be seen inwardly as light and heard by the inner ear as sound. Thus the name, Light and Sound.

The Masters of Light and Sound state that God personified does not exist within Its creation, which includes the many universes and planes of existence. However, through the Audible Life Stream, the Holy Spirit that is universally present and active, the Creator can remain within Its creation without being a specific part of it. Through the Audible Life Stream, the Divine can contact, control, and sustain all life within Its universal body.

Many seekers of truth who practice meditation or some types of yoga have experiences in which they may see streaks or flashes of many-colored lights. These experiences are manifestations of the light which exists in both the outer physical worlds and the inner worlds. This spiritual light abounds on the physical plane of reality in various forms—sunlight, artificial light created by electricity, fire, or lightning. All forms of energy on the physical plane are derivatives of this light of God.

Other forms of light, such as ultraviolet and infrared light, also exist on the physical plane, yet are invisible to our unaided physical senses. The same principle applies in regard to the inner light, which shines constantly within our finer bodies, yet remains unseen by our physical eyes. Seekers who have experiences with the inner light do so in periods of meditation when the physical senses are subdued, giving rise to the heightened awareness of the senses of the astral body, which can perceive this inner light.

Other than just the pure majesty of witnessing a beautiful sunset or the captivating experience of seeing the inner light, what does the light represent in spiritual terms? When people say, "I see the light!" they are not alluding to the physical light and certainly not to the inner light, but to a particular point of view or understanding. They are saying that something now makes sense to them because they have new information or knowledge that allows them to form a relationship between two previously separate ideas. Metaphysically, the darkness was turned into light.

The esoteric, hidden meaning of the Light of God means knowledge and information to the spiritual seeker of truth. When we study religions, science, metaphysics, astrology, tarot, or philosophy, we are seeking information and knowledge of the divine workings. Our mental and emotional senses are highly stimulated by such study, and we feel a new lightness of being within as we grow in knowledge of our relationship to the Divine. These pursuits of the light are important, and indeed gratifying, when compared to living in the dark, or having interest only in purely physical pursuits and gratifications. Still, when the light has served its purpose in our spiritual development, the Sound appears.

Religious, shamanistic, and native ceremonies throughout the world reveal the importance that all cultures and beliefs place on the role of sound and the Sound Current. Chanting, drumming, bells, horns, flutes, and singing are used worldwide to help humans commune with the god of their understanding. Sound is the basic, original element of the Light and Sound aspects of the Audible Life Stream. All the outer worlds of God, as well as all the inner planes of experience, reverberate continually with the Divine Melody. This spiritual fact has been recognized worldwide by nearly all religions and native systems of belief. Almost all great religious texts and sacred writings refer to the audibility of spirit as it flows from the Godhead to give life and consciousness to the creation. As spirit flows through the various planes of experience, it creates a vibration in the atmosphere of each world, which can be heard by the auditory senses of each of our five bodies.

The Light and Sound teachings place great importance on the audibility of spirit because of the nature of the Sound Current Itself. This Current's two main aspects actually resemble a great wave of motion and sound. Its first aspect is the out-flowing, circular wave which emerges from the Godhead to sustain life on all planes of experience. The second aspect is the returning wave, which returns through the created worlds and back into the bosom of God.

The primary spiritual exercise by which the seeker can experience the Audible Life Stream involves centering one's attention at the third-eye center. As this is accomplished, the student begins to perceive the Divine Melody of the universe's sounds with the inner senses, hearing buzzing bees, tinkling bells, rushing water, harps, flutes, and even bagpipes. Each specific sound relates to a specific vibration which the wave of spirit creates as it passes through the many planes of inner experiences. This great Sound Current provides a stream of spirit for the spiritual seeker to tune into and experience the inner dimensions of consciousness.

The soul body has senses, as do all the other bodies within our being. These senses are referred to by the Masters as the "seeing" and "hearing" qualities of soul. "Seeing" refers to soul's ability to see and know truth instantly. Soul's seeing provides a clear picture of reality from the overview of soul, which is separate from our likes and dislikes and from what the mind believes to be true. It is our highest faculty of awareness. Have you ever experienced an instant of total clarity when you just knew what the truth was in a given situation? This is the seeing faculty of soul in action; it does not use logic, reason, or emotion in its seeing but acts with direct perception. Of course, trying to understand this faculty of soul from the mental point of view boggles the mind. We never will be able to do so because the seeing faculty of soul exists in a higher, finer band of reality than our thought processes.

Soul also possesses the inner faculty of hearing—the ability to perceive the divine sounds echoing within all of us, sounds that the physical senses cannot hear. Before this divine faculty can be activated, we must gather our scattered attention from the outside world and redirect it to the third-eye center, the gateway to the inner planes of experience. Until we make such preparations, our contact with the Audible Life Stream will be very spotty or non-existent.

The Audible Life Stream is much more than pleasing sounds to the inner ear. This Sound Current is actually a divine river of consciousness that contains all the God-like attributes of love, wisdom, freedom, and power. The esoteric or genuine meaning of the Sound Current far exceeds Its apparent meaning. When bathing in this river of God, we begin to realize and actualize these God-attributes within ourselves. As we come into greater contact and experience with the latent qualities of soul, new vistas open up before us, and understanding and the power to actuate our spiritual growth and unfoldment increase dramatically. All of these realizations are the result of higher consciousness manifesting within the seeker, enlivened by contact with the Audible Life Stream.

The pursuit of knowledge and spiritual information is important in the beginning phases of seekers' quests, but the progression from the light element of awareness to the superior gifts of the Sound element will deliver us to our anticipated goal. Working with the light can produce temporary relief from physical, emotional, or mental anguish and limitations; yet the pain always returns. While one set of limiting circumstances may be removed when we attempt to heal ourselves through the aid of the light alone, sooner or later another set of equally limiting barriers will replace it. For example, one may give up drugs, only to replace them with alcohol or food; or one may renounce greed, only to fall prey to vanity induced by a false sense of accomplishment. In seeking the light, the true peace and contentment we desire remains elusive; and the frustrations born of such partial results become our daily companion.

Again, much more than listening to beautiful sounds or music, spiritual attunement to the Sound Current within is the process for liberating soul from the clutches of mind, emotion, and illusion. This way of spiritual attainment and enlightenment far outstrips what can be gained spiritually through following the spiritual energy of the light. While information and knowledge—the fruits of pursuing the light—provide relative levels of peace and spiritual progress, they pale in comparison to the higher God attributes of true love, wisdom, freedom, and power which the awakened Sound Current imbues within the sincere seeker of truth. These divine attributes, which are enlivened through bathing in the Audible Life Stream, transform the seeker of truth into a doer of truth.

The Sound can heal the deep-seated karmic conditions that limit all seekers and keep us from experiencing the contact with the God within, which we so fervently desire. Where the light can reveal truth to the seeker's eyes, the Sound actualizes what the light reveals.

The explanation of this lies in the light itself. Originating in the mental body and stationed and active within the energy centers of our physical bodies, the light element of the Audible Life Stream deals with thought, feeling, and personal will. Although these are powerful and important faculties to have at our disposal, they pale in comparison to the faculties of soul. Healings which come through a change of mind or feeling, instigated by personal will, simply do not have the sustaining power to be permanent or complete. True healings require the action and true transformational ability of Sound.

Sound lies within the heart of God. Sound is the most powerful force in all creation, carrying with It the power to transform. Sound replaces our illusions with truth. It is pure consciousness itself, the source of all lasting, creative endeavors, and the deliverer of soul. It is indeed the force which liberates the beautiful butterfly of soul from its cocoon, freeing soul to live and unfold in a way heretofore unexperienced and only vaguely conceived.

We remain "seekers" of spiritual reality and not "finders," as long as the light, not the Sound, is the basis of our search. While light is powerful and necessary in its own realm (including mind, emotions, and ego), soul's awakening is not completed through the energies of light. Sound is the spiritual energy that enlivens soul, not the mind. Awakening the Sound Current awakens the essence of soul, and all life changes for the seeker.

The stunning simplicity of the Sound energy confounds the mind. We are conditioned to use mind to solve all of life's dilemmas, unaware that the latent energy of Sound, once released, provides the permanent solution of awakened spiritual living—removing the necessity to rely on mind, feelings, or intuition. The spiritual energies of both light and Sound are vast and complex, but in essence they are very simple.

How big is your well?

CHAPTER 2

REGAINING THE THRONE

Despite the efforts of great masters, spiritual teachers, and mystics, humankind still remains basically ignorant of our true spiritual makeup and unique capabilities. The great strides made in science, medicine, and technology serve to benefit only our physical existence and to make our outer, earthly life more comfortable. Organized religion, which supposedly exists to bring spiritual enlightenment and fulfillment, has not made such strides. In fact, many major religions of the world presently appear to be on the downslide while the general public's interest in spiritual and psychic matters steadily increases.

This condition can only be resolved by great effort at spiritual self-examination, the inward journey of soul. Many of us have reached a point in our unfoldment where we are no longer fully satisfied by learning more about the physical world and its workings, nor by devoting great amounts of time and energy to our bodily comforts and well being. Our need for spiritual truth and the accompanying desire to live closer to the God within outstrips our interest in discovering more about our external environment.

Recognizing ourselves as soul and living through this identification is simple—but not easy. We are composed of five distinct levels of consciousness, and to reach our true identity we must first recognize and then assimilate both the values and limitations of the lower four. This all-important journey is filled with seductive detours and outright dangers. Only by recognizing all that we are not can we begin to know who we truly are—soul—and experience living from this transcendental perspective. Only thus do we regain the throne and realize our true spiritual inheritance.

The Five Bodies and Their Corresponding Planes

> *In my Father's house are many mansions. (John 14:2)*
>
> *The Kingdom of Heaven is within you. (Luke 17:21)*
>
> Jesus
Master of Light and Sound

> *When I learned the lesson of Love,*
> *   my mind rebelled against church and mosque.*
> *I entered the real Temple of the Lord*
> *   where a thousand instruments played.*
> *I found my Beloved in my house.*
>
> Bulleh Shah
18th century Muslim saint
Disciple of Shah Inayat

To more fully understand and enliven our contact with the Kingdom of God which exists within, we must explore and understand our own makeup as spiritual beings.

Through our five bodies—the physical, astral, causal, mental, and soul bodies—we possess the ability to gain great knowledge of our physical world as well as the dimensions of consciousness that lie within, corresponding to these five bodies. The great religions, indigenous belief systems throughout the world, and even metaphysics refer to these inner levels of the heavens. Although the names change from culture to culture and place to place, all recognize this inner reality of God's kingdom. For example, the physical body is limited to experiencing life in the physical world. It cannot recognize nor live life beyond the veil because its rate of vibration does not match that of any of the inner worlds, only that of the physical world. The astral body operates on the next plane of existence—the astral plane. The causal body matches the vibrations of the causal plane, which are somewhat higher and finer than those of the astral body. The mental body vibrates at a rate which corresponds to the mental plane of existence. Finally, the soul body vibrates in harmony with the rate of vibration we encounter on the soul plane. These five bodies of humans and the five corresponding spiritual planes are shown on pages 16 and 17. This brief look is greatly simplified, as each plane contains many subplanes and regions we will not discuss here. In addition, even more subtle dimensions of experience are said to exist beyond the soul plane.

Our first body, the physical body, is the one with which we are most familiar. It has five main senses and is subject to the physical laws of our universe, including birth and death. Although science tells us that it is made up mostly of water, the Masters say that all life is part of the universal body of God! Therefore, all life and all matter are made of God's essence—what we often refer to as spirit. Matter is only spirit vibrating at an extremely low rate so it appears to be solid. Other dimensions of existence, which lie beyond our physical senses, differ from the physical world because their frequency or rate of vibration is much higher than that of the physical world. Matter becomes less dense and more refined as we penetrate other planes of experience (often called the heavens, the afterlife, or the worlds beyond the veil).

All things express their inherent spiritual nature through their rates of vibration. Don't we all experience different thoughts, feelings, or impulses at different locations in our physical world? The inspiration and majesty of the high mountains, the roaring waterfall, the raging sea; the introspective quality of the calm lake, the vast desert, or the gently rolling hills are determined by the amount of spirit present. When we hear people say, "I really liked the vibes there," or that a person or place has "good vibes," it expresses our sensitivity to the spirit of that place, person, or thing.

The Five Human Bodies
Within the physical being

Soul Body
True Identity
Spiritual Senses:
  Knowing
  Being
  Seeing
  Direct Perception

Thought Body
Mental Senses:
  Reason
  Intellect
  Logic

Seed Body
Karmic Records Stored
Causal Senses:
  Action & Reaction
  Law of Cause & Effect

Light Body
Astral Senses:
  Emotional Feelings
  Imaginative Power
  Instinctive Behavior

Human Body
Physical Senses
  Touch
  Taste
  Smell
  Sight
  Hearing

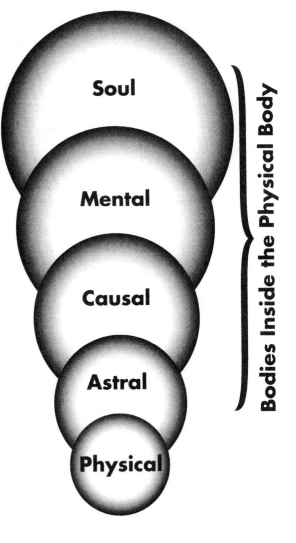

Bodies Inside the Physical Body

Five Major Spiritual Planes
Accessed through the third eye

Soul Plane
Kingdom of Heaven
God Realization
Origin of the Audible Life Stream

Mental Plane
Highest Mind
Mental Body • Cosmic Consciousness
Source of Religion & Philosophy

Causal Plane
Karma (Cause & Effect) – Past, Present, Future
Seed Body
Karmic Records Stored

Astral Plane
Psychic Phenomena
Astral Travel • Emotional Body –
Source of Imaginative Faculty

Physical Plane
Soul Encumbered by Mind & Senses
Physical Body

Everything in the physical world is composed of spirit and, being part of the universal body of God, is alive. Perhaps not alive in the sense that the biological sciences describe life, but very alive in the sense that the Masters describe life. The mineral kingdom is composed of spirit, just as we are, but at a much lower rate of vibration and with considerably fewer modes of expression than we humans possess. The Masters say that if spirit is present, as it must be in all things for them to exist, then both consciousness and awareness are also present. All rocks, minerals, and gems have their own quantity of spirit, with their particular rate of vibration. We find certain minerals or gems more appealing than others due to their higher rates of vibration, which give them the particular structures, colors, patterns, or brilliance that we find attractive.

The mineral state of consciousness has not developed mental or emotional states such as we have, yet does it not react to heat, cold, light, and sound? Its particular atomic structure allows expansion and contraction as it grows and bonds to other minerals. The rock or mineral state of consciousness experiences life only through its physical body. Changes such as expansion and contraction, extrusion and erosion reflect its way of expressing itself. Thus, the experience of life in the mineral state is vastly different than ours, due to its physical makeup or constitution.

The more complex a life form is, the greater becomes its ability to express the spirit within. Plants can respond not only to the physical world as minerals can, but apparently they can respond emotionally as well. They appear to prefer certain lights, sounds, and human beings more than others. The animal kingdom is noticeably more developed in terms of emotional response, for the element of intelligence enters the picture. By the time we come to the human being, we also see the potential for spirit to be expressed in varied forms, from the miserable to the sublime. This enormous potential for variety in human experience and expression exists because we are five-bodied beings with the infinite potential for creating our own reality.

Our next body, the astral body, deals largely with the whole band of emotional expression and feelings such as personal love, joy, anger, and fear. Certain psychics and clairvoyants can read the emotional makeup of an individual by expressions and body language in the astral body, in much the same way as we can read the physical body. The astral plane, the realm of experience which corresponds in vibration to the astral body, is a region of brilliant light, angelic realms, and beautiful sounds, as well as negative entities, black magic, and Satanism. Upon the death of the physical body, soul will take up life on this plane, using the astral body as its primary vehicle. After a period of time in the astral world, soul reincarnates again into the physical worlds.

All the feelings and emotions that originate within our astral bodies can be extremely valuable or detrimental to our spiritual life. Haven't we all experienced the paralyzing effects of fears? Fear of a new job, a new boss, moving, entering school, or leaving school can immobilize us and keep us from experiencing what life has in store for us and what soul may need as a next step in discovering itself. For instance, how can soul's voice be heard if it is time to move and we are unduly attached to our apartment or current location? On the other hand, a little healthy fear, such as fear of attachment, goes a long way toward assisting us in our spiritual journey and allowing us to remain open to soul's constant urgings.

The third body, the causal body, holds a complete record of the experiences, thoughts, words, and deeds that form the character for our present life. Our body type, race, mental and emotional make-up, and experiences in life are largely determined by our past actions, or karma. This body is less dense than the astral body and has a vibration similar to the causal plane of experience. The causal body deals largely with the principle of cause and effect: herein lies the individual's karmic record. Our present and previous thoughts, words, and deeds put a particular cause into motion; and all these causes create specific effects. The great law of karma requires that all life must eventually come into harmony, so as Jesus taught, we must reap the rewards and punishments of all the seeds we have sown.

Many psychics, fortune tellers, and those who deal with past-life readings get their data from the causal plane of experience. Those who work in this field authentically are able to shift their attention to the causal body, and thereby tune into the time track records of past, present, and future located on the causal plane.

Our fourth body, the mental body from which all mental faculties originate and in which thought, logic, reason, perspective, and ego are born, is the body with which we all identify so strongly. This is the home of the ego and the personality, the mental arena that creates all our prized identifications by which we define ourselves. These identifications of the ego and personality are all false gods because our true identity exists only within soul; it is our misuse of the mental faculties that allows soul to be held in bondage by the mind. Thus the mind can be our worst enemy as well as our great friend.

The mental body is quite susceptible to the five passions of the mind—lust, vanity, greed, anger, and attachment. Left unchecked, these passions of the mind poison the mental body and keep the higher spiritual intentions of soul from penetrating our consciousness by keeping our attention focused on the external world where we constantly seek pleasures and avoid pain. These passions keep us locked into our many false identifications and beliefs, and protect the ego and the personality from being exposed for what they are.

The essence of the spiritual journey of soul is to turn the mind around so it will look to soul for guidance, wisdom, freedom, and love, rather than allowing it to look through the physical senses to the external world for its pleasure and gratification. When the seeker trains the mind to see things in a spiritual light rather than through the ego and the personality, the mind becomes the seeker's great ally in discovering spiritual truth and reality. Thought, reason, and logic either support or deny our spiritual journey and our daily experiences as a soul within the physical body.

The mental plane of experience, corresponding with the mental body, is a world of stupefying beauty and light, the source of inspiration for many sacred writings, philosophies, and moral teachings. This stunning region of the inner worlds is also home to the universal mind where soul, on its initial journey from the bosom of the Divine, picks up its individual mind as it continues its journey to an incarnation in the physical worlds. After eons of experience in the physical worlds, soul becomes spiritualized to the point where it begins to return to the Godhead, its original home. On this return journey, it will again come to the area of the mental worlds where the universal mind originated. Then, because it will no longer have use for its mental apparatus, it will leave the individual mind in the mental plane and continue its inward journey in the soul body.

Our fifth body is the soul body, made in the image and form of the Creator. The soul body, in which all are created equal, is our highest nature and our true, hidden identity. It does not experience death as do all the other bodies, and its essence is the same as that of God. Therefore, it is imbued with the God-like qualities of unconditional love, wisdom, power, and freedom. We experience real objectivity through the soul body, without the prejudices of the mind.

These five bodies represent distinct levels of awareness within our being. We live in these five bodies both separately and simultaneously in any given moment of the day. Our faculty of attention, a quality of soul, determines which of our bodies is employed at any given moment. Soul, our most sublime faculty and true identity, becomes trapped within these lower bodies due to our own failures to monitor our attention. In fact, through thousands of lifetimes, we have become so hypnotically entrenched in viewing life through the lens of the lower bodies' viewpoints that we fail to see the forest for the trees. The grandeur of the mighty landscape of our perception fixates on the parts at the expense of the whole—soul.

Soul is constantly looking out at the world, gathering perceptions and images. It views the world through the lens of the particular body in which the attention is stationed. For example, if our predominant makeup is to view the world and life emotionally, we give great attention to our feelings, likes, and dislikes, allowing our emotions to dominate our points of view and behaviors. Occasionally soul can be recognized in certain dreams, visions, moments of inspiration, or intuitive flashes.

Our overwhelming concern with our physical well-being, desires, and the passions of the mind (lust, vanity, anger, greed, attachment) has scattered our attention out into the physical world so completely that precious little energy remains to activate our innate faculties of soul. The process is reversible for those with an ardent desire to see soul regain the throne of rulership and experience the spiritual reality of self-realization:

> *It can therefore be said that the purpose of life is to first discover who you are. Everyone thinks they know who they are, but this is*

only a case of thought, produced by the programming of our culture. These false identities are stripped, as soul ascends in consciousness through the many planes. It must be remembered that these other bodies are only present to protect soul from the coarse vibrations, and to gather impressions and expressions on each relative plane with the respective body. When these necessary experiences are gathered, the lower bodies are no longer needed. Reason and logic no longer suffice, nor do the explanations of the clergy seem to clarify anything. Only when soul, in and of Itself, can view life for what it really is, can the seeker claim that he or she knows self. At this point, one will say that "I am soul; I am not the mind or the physical body."

Sri Gary Olsen
1948 –
Author and Master of Light and Sound

The soul plane corresponds in vibration with the soul body. The Masters of Light and Sound speak little of the glorious worlds of the soul plane, except that they are regions of unimaginable beauty and sounds. At this level of consciousness, the souls who have entered this region live peacefully and in bliss and harmony. Little, if any, discord exists, and soul is free to use the divine energy of God to create its own lifespace in the present moment. Many souls who reach the soul plane and experience God realization (unity with the God essence within them) return to the many dimensions, galaxies, and universes of the lower worlds to carry on the great work of the Creator in one form or another.

The Law of Karma

Nowhere has the law of karma been more simply or eloquently described than in the statement, "As ye sow, so shall ye reap." The law of karma, also known as the law of cause and effect, simply means that all thoughts, words, and deeds are acts of creation; and all such creation brings a response, or effect.

The Western world has long suffered under misinterpretations that some religious establishments have made regarding the law of karma, replacing it with the concept of sin and moral behavior.

Both sin and correct behavior have been codified and given moralistic values, with the final reckoning of these accounts placed in the future, on the judgment day. These rewards and punishments, administered by an external source, hinder the spiritual development of our society. Our citizens have become increasingly guilt-ridden, paranoid, reactionary, and violent.

The law of karma incorporates no punishment or reward; it exists only to teach responsibility for one's creations. The seeker should view this spiritual law as a gift from God, meant to bring all life into greater recognition of, and harmony with, its Creator.

We cannot separate the subject of karma from the topic of reincarnation. Karma holds all the lower worlds (physical, astral, causal, and mental) together. The thread of karma weaves together insects, plants, animals, humans, nations, planets, solar systems, universes, and entire planes of experience. It is so strong that it seems unbreakable, yet it is so fine that it is seldom seen. Our minds, thoughts, attitudes, emotions, and physical bodies constantly create karma. The law of karma allows each of us to learn the great universal principles that govern us all through observation, experience, and trial and error, enabling each soul to come into harmony with them by allowing the individual to experience many lives in many bodies. In fact, seekers must live millions of lifetimes, in many forms, to bring their karmas into a state of balance. Until we learn to live without creating karma, we will continue to reincarnate into the lower worlds. As long as we have any credits to collect or debts due to the world, we remain here for the maturation of soul.

All life seeks balance, and the great law of karma supports and enforces this principle. Most seekers readily see and accept the reality of negative karma. We realize that deceit, manipulation, dishonesty, and anger will return to us so we can experience the effect of our ill-considered creation. For example, perhaps in a previous incarnation you were a man in a position of power who abused authority and were particularly critical and mean-spirited toward women. According to the law of karma, it will be necessary for you to experience, for yourself, the effects of these causes which you previously set into motion. You will find yourself incarnating into a female body and experiencing the wrath of an abusive male authority figure who makes your life miserable. Ideally, the results of this situation will be more remedial than punitive.

Our positive actions in thought, word, and deed also bring an equal response or effect from life itself; thus, some are born into favorable circumstances while others appear destined for a life of suffering and deprivation. It is only our karmic accounts that spawn all conditions we experience within our present lifetime. Many use their good karma to amass wealth, live in luxury, eat fine foods, and fulfill all the desires of the physical senses. As true spiritual seekers we may realize that our spiritual funds can be used much more wisely, and so we go about the business of seeking liberation, setting our feet firmly on the path of the divine journey of soul.

To assume that we are totally free agents in this world reveals a lack of understanding of karma. Yet most individuals, and even many seekers, live under the illusion of free will. We feel that we, as individuals, make choices in the moment which determine the course of our lives. We believe that we choose our jobs, mates, location, etc.; in reality, our karma determines where and when we are born, who our parents are, where we live, our profession, mate, and even our children. Our karma, through heredity, determines our body type and size, our health, and our moment of departure from this earthly incarnation. All these choices are made in the astral worlds, prior to the present incarnation, before we enter our present body. Our previous karma builds, molds, and forms the lessons, experiences, and length of the present lifetime.

Liberation is not for the few, the chosen, the select. It is for all when they cease to create karma. It is you yourselves who set in motion this wheel of birth and death whose spokes are agonies and pains and it is you alone who can stop that wheel so it turns no more. Then you are free. Most people cling to this individuality, this sense of I. It is that which creates karma. Liberation is life and the cessation of life. It is as a great fire and when you enter it you become the flame, and then you go forth as sparks, part of that flame.

Krishnamurti
1895 – 1986
Mystic, author, lecturer

The will to liberation cannot be born until seekers become extremely weary of this life, consumed by slavery and bondage to the law of karma. From soul's elevated viewpoint, all its personalities live at once and are synthesized in the current incarnation; so as spiritual seekers, we must understand that we are as we are simply because of our karma. All our mechanical reactions and judgments of the world, all our notions of superiority or inferiority, all our self-seeking goals pursued at the expense of others are part of the chains of karma which bind us to the human consciousness and stand between the "I" of ego and the true spiritual self.

The sincere seeker must come to see that the law of karma binds us to human consciousness with both iron shackles and golden chains. Many seekers are aware that anger, fear, selfishness, and greed are negative states of being which create negative karma. However, don't we all make judgments based on what we feel is good or right and react positively to such judgments? Generally we are conditioned to smile easily, be friendly and sociable, and come to the aid of those who need help. Individuals who define this positive behavior as correct often become rescuers and people pleasers—kind and charitable people. While such behavior is neither good nor bad in and of itself, it does have effects. Such people-pleasing, rescuing behaviors can deprive others of their karmic lessons and the opportunity of taking responsibility for their own behavior. In such cases, the law of karma forges golden chains—the bond of positive karma—between the parties involved in such well-intentioned helpfulness.

These positive and negative states of being are conditions of the mind, emotions, and personality which create all karma; they rely on our mental conditioning, value system, and personal judgment for validity. On the other hand, soul identification transcends karma because it exists beyond the dual currents, the positive and negative states of being, which control the lower worlds and the lower bodies. Soul's direct perception allows us to see everything in life non-judgmentally; it does not engage in positive or negative judgment in thought or emotion. Soul is fully aware that nothing in the lower worlds escapes the law of cause and effect. Its unique viewpoint brings forth understanding and compassion for all life, without judgment, because it can perceive situations as they truly are and experience life in freedom, joy, and spiritual bliss, without the need for responding positively or negatively.

All human beings, as souls, have this innate quality and capability within them. This spiritual consciousness represents centered action—soul's level of understanding and viewpoint. Human consciousness represents attachment to positive and negative thoughts or emotions, and bondage to the earth. Seekers must be aware of the difference between soul and their thoughts, feelings, ideas, and personality formed by the law of karma. Soul needs the human state of awareness and its karmic lessons to first discover what it is not and then to be free, wise, loving, and powerful in expressing all that it truly is.

The Miracle of the Moment

> *Let us forget the lapse of time;*
> *let us forget the conflict of opinions.*
> *Let us make our appeal to the infinite,*
> *and take up our positions there.*

Chuang Tzu
ca. 369 – 286 B.C.
Taoist sage

> *The absolute tranquility of the present moment.*
> *Though it is at this moment, there is no limit*
> *to this moment, and herein are eternal delights.*

Hui-neng
638 – 713
The Sixth Zen Patriarch

> *In the spiritual world there are no time divisions such as the past, present, and future; for they have contracted themselves into a single moment of the present where life quivers in its true sense...the past and the future are both rolled up in this moment of the present moment of illumination, and this present moment is not something standing still with all its contents, for it ceaselessly moves on.*

D. T. Suzuki
1869 – 1966
Author, lecturer, and Buddhist scholar

Can the chains of karma be broken? Yes! Does humankind have any free will? Yes! Can we change the occurrence and outcome of events? Yes! Indeed we can! As spiritual beings we are destined to do so. Just as the caterpillar must leave the life of an earthbound creature and become the beautiful being of flight, so too do we begin to sense the freedom awaiting us as the chains of karma loosen. As truth seekers, we can take responsibility for our divine faculties of choice, imagination, and creation. Our first responsibility is recognizing and facing the karmic situations we have brought to the moment, without identifying ourselves as our karma but rather as a soul experiencing life events we have created.

The greatest limitation of the human state of consciousness is its failure to recognize its true origin. We have been duped through illusion and self-hypnosis into believing that we are our thoughts, rather than soul expressing thought and intelligence through the mind. We have been cleverly hoodwinked into believing that we are our emotions and feelings, rather than knowing we are soul using the emotional body to experience feelings. We have accepted the notion that we are a physical body with a gender, a level of education, a profession, and a given karmic experience—rather than realizing that we are soul, inhabiting a physical body. Ultimately we have created our karma to experience just who we are and to know what a magnificently powerful and creative entity soul is.

Bringing soul into its rightful position of control and authority within the five bodies of our constitutions deals directly with choice, free will, creativity, and the power of imagination. All these God-given qualities of expression are intimately related to the present moment of time—the miracle of the moment. We can only use our creative and imaginative faculties right now—not at any other time. We may use our imagination and creativity to delve into the past or to mold the future by our present attitudes and our positive spiritual imaging. Nevertheless, all these actions can only be done in the present moment.

The hustle and bustle of the human state of consciousness, with its frenzied pursuit of pleasure and avoidance of pain, leaves little time or attention to experience the miracle of the moment. If we closely monitor our attention and witness the parade of inner thoughts, we will see that we are deeply attached to what has been and filled with anxiety and anticipation about what is to come. The present moment, the only point in time that matters, is submerged like a boulder in the raging river that is our stream of consciousness.

Interest in the past and the future indicates that our mind, emotions, and ego are in control. Only the ego gets sustenance and nourishment from what has been or what is to come; it loves nostalgia, the comfort of the past, and has grave concern for its survival in the future. The emotions supportively surround our memories of past accomplishment and success with warm feelings and instill fear into our view of the future. The mind reviews the past to prepare for the future and to ensure the ego's survival in happiness and comfort. Our minds and egos, if required to dwell in the present, often experience great pain. All the exposed inadequacies and shortcomings of the little self come rushing to the surface. When we attempt to still the mind, it immediately rushes out in a thousand directions, truly afraid to face itself for fear of what it might see.

The present is the true home of soul and the breeding ground of its desires. These propensities of the lower bodies to avoid the present moment are warnings to us. Most of us are not nearly as happy or content as we pretend to be, for human consciousness knows no true contentment—only soul does. The moment, the now, the present is as pervasive to soul as it is elusive to the mind. Soul always lives in the moment, never in the past nor in the future. It is the background across which the mind races in its attempt to escape the moment; it is timeless, ever-present, and ever-now.

Within the sphere of activity of a spiritual student, soul is first cause. It is as a spark is to the flame, a drop is to the ocean, and a grain of sand is to the beach. We, as soul, enliven the moment and experience the miracle of life or consciousness itself. The mind and all the lower bodies, even the physical body, reflect soul's ability to create. The dilemma that seekers face when entering into the spiritual life is, "Which creations will be allowed to manifest and become real, and what do I have to leave behind as I pursue greater purity?"

The supreme challenge for the spiritual seeker always lies within the present moment of time. Within this moment lies the potential for spiritual unfoldment and growth, or the potential for increasing the burden of karma through the unrestrained thoughts, feelings, and the conditioned reactions of the lower bodies. Remember, each of our five bodies has its desires and abilities to create. It is imperative that the seeker becomes highly aware of the creative nature of each of these five bodies and seizes the opportunity of choice and creativity that only the present moment allows. Should we fall asleep and fail to monitor our attention, we will find that karma will automatically come into play. The reactive, mechanical, pre-conditioned natures of the lower bodies unfailingly react to present circumstances as their past conditioning demands; this is not freedom, this is karma. As long as soul's perspective is kept from illuminating the present moment, karma will be our master.

The chains of karma *can* be broken. This opportunity of genuine, creative action within the present moment is the key to liberation. All the methods, disciplines, and teachings of the Masters are directed to bringing the student into the present moment. We create our reality through our points of attention and the attitudes that accompany them. Any theory we may have regarding the potency and potential of the moment is valueless unless our attention is in the moment and our point of view is that of soul, and not of the mind or ego.

The Masters stress the need for conscious balance within our lives so our sensory desires don't rule us, and for contentment and detachment so we can willingly forego excesses in pleasures and transmute pain into understanding. They teach self-control so we may enter into and come to master the miracle of the moment, resulting in conscious, loving creations.

The law of karma exists simply for us to become aware of our intentions and to become responsible for them. Because all karma deals with cause and effect, cause is inseparable from our intentions; every thought, word, and deed has its intention. Some of our intentions are noble and are motivated by the higher thoughts or points of view of the human consciousness; others are not so pure. Because soul's qualities and intentions are one with God's, there is no difference between its actions (causes) and their ensuing effects. Both are divinely ordained, so how can soul, as one with the Creator, act apart from it? No karma—positive or negative—is created when soul's intentions manifest.

For example, suppose a boating accident occurs when a dock worker fails to properly check out our rented sailboat (after he returns from lunch inebriated), and our tiller snaps off when we are miles away from the dock. If the negative intentions or causes of the mind manifest, we will be angry, indignant, feel like a victim, and probably become self-righteous and vindictive. If we take no responsibility for the accident, but place the blame solely on the worker, judging him to be incompetent and irresponsible, we simultaneously increase our karmic burden. Should our positive intentions manifest, we will have sympathy for ourselves as the unwary victims and sympathy for the dock worker's situation. We probably will project our kind feelings onto him and imagine him to be concerned, sorry, and in the process of penance and change. Whether this is true or not, our intentions will be to hope that it is true. We will see him as essentially a good man who had a rough day and who deserves our sympathy. Either of these scenarios of judgment increases the pre-existing bond of karma between the dock worker and ourselves, which brought on the accident in the first place.

If soul's intentions control the incident on the lake, then the scenario will be one of soul's action rather than the karma-producing reactions of the lower bodies. Through the spiritualized lens of soul, we will see that the accident was no accident at all, but an opportunity for growth and understanding for all involved; and we will not shirk our responsibility for having created the situation, whether we have been at fault or not. The "seeing" faculty of soul will recognize the situation for what it is without judging ourselves or the dock worker. His part in the accident may bring civil or legal effects to him, for which he is responsible; but soul does not see him as incompetent and irresponsible—only as soul. And as soul, we will have compassion and forgiveness for him, directed to him as soul. Soul's wisdom, understanding, and divine love allow it to act in such a way that no karma is accrued as a result of its actions. Soul always acts for the benefit of the whole, not the individual parts. Its knowledge of divine justice ensures that by acting from the overview of soul, we bring greater love and understanding to all situations than we could possibly bring from any viewpoint, positive or negative, within the mind.

The past has brought us to the circumstances we experience in the moment. The miracle of the moment lies within our choice, freedom, and power to act in a way that brings spiritual upliftment to ourselves and all life. The choice is always ours, in every moment.

The Role of the Master

> *Find thou a mystic guide, for beset with*
> *dangers is this journey for whosoever*
> *without the Master ventures on the path...*

Rumi
13th century Muslim saint of Persia
Master of Light and Sound

There is no greater day in the life of a seeker than the day our karma brings us to a true Master. Although we may be mentally unaware of the lifetimes of preparation which have brought us to this moment, in soul we are fully aware. Generally, upon meeting a genuine Master, the seeker experiences undeniable upliftment, magnetic attraction to, and a feeling of love for the Master, and a sense of well-being that seems to come from within. This meeting of the student with the Master exemplifies the spiritual fact that the past always creates the present moment.

Many seekers who become aware of the Light and Sound teachings are confused about the role of the Master. First of all, just what does the word "Master" mean? A spiritual Master of Light and Sound is a man or woman who has experienced the inner journey of self-discovery and attained both self-realization and God realization —union with the soul and the God within us all. Therefore, the Master is able to directly manifest the qualities of soul and spirit. A conduit for the Divine, the Master directly manifests the love, wisdom, power, and freedom of the Lord. Upon meeting such individuals, you often sense their divine nature immediately. A true Master radiates warmth, love, beauty, and truth in a way that most of us have never before experienced.

A Parable

Peter the Great, the Czar, wanted to learn shipbuilding; and he wanted to bring this knowledge to Russia. There wasn't much shipbuilding going on in Russia, and no one knew very much about it, so Peter decided to go to Holland where shipbuilding was a fine art. Being a Czar and rather well-known, he couldn't just walk into Holland and get all the secrets, so he made himself look like a common laborer. He talked like a laborer, he dressed like a laborer, and he went to Holland. He got a job in the shipyards and stayed for years, studying shipbuilding, learning everything he could. Being the wonderful, wise man and ruler that he was, many of the other laborers, artisans, craftspeople, and engineers in Holland were very impressed with him, and he attracted a lot of friends.

When the time came for Peter to return to Russia, a lot of people grieved. They had come to love this man and did not want him to leave, but Peter said, "It's time for me to go home."

"What do you mean, 'home,' Peter? Aren't you a laborer, a shipbuilder?"

And Peter just said, "It's time to go home, and I'm leaving."

Some of them liked Peter so well that they decided to go with him; and so, off they went. Well, traveling with Peter was quite a blessing. The closer they got to Russia, the better things got. They would show up at a farm and all of a sudden, chickens and lambs would be killed, the best corn would come out, festive baking was done, the best wine was uncorked. In the next town, the inn was thrown open; the travelers had the best rooms and anything they wanted. There was no more sleeping in barns. This was quite a blessed journey. Still the travelers did not know with whom they traveled.

Finally they got to Russia. At this point, people were bowing in the streets, prostrating themselves before the Czar, welcoming him. Finally the travelers started to get an idea of what was going on. When they finally arrived in the capital, there were great parades and great joy that the Czar was back home in his homeland. Then the travelers truly understood the nature of the Czar and their journey, and they were all given kingdoms and made princes and princesses.

Traveling with a genuine spiritual Master is much like traveling with Czar Peter—the Master is needed mainly because of his familiarity with the territory. The Master is one who has completed the journey of soul that the student is only beginning. Soul's job is to master karma by mastering the moment, every moment. However, soul is so entrapped by karma in the four lower bodies, it cannot do this successfully without the aid and guidance of a living Master. The Master brings great experience, awareness, and compassionate sensitivity to the relationship with the student. This experience is invaluable in helping students over the many rocky shoals they will no doubt encounter on the spiritual journey. The relationship the student forms with the Master is similar to other relationships in life where a more experienced individual lends assistance and expertise to another person—the master/apprentice relationship in trades and art guilds or the intern/doctor relationship in hospitals. In life, we constantly rely on the wisdom of past generations, our elders, or more experienced individuals because it is wise to do so.

The same logic applies to the spiritual journey of self-realization and God realization. The journey to self-realization—discovering and actualizing one's true identity as soul—makes most worldly projects look like child's play. It is a journey of many dead ends, false summits, box canyons, and blind alleys. Without the experienced guiding hand of the Master to assist and point the way, one's chances are nearly zero. The necessity of the Master lies in his or her supreme competency in bringing the students to their goals.

"I point the way; you walk the path" best sums up the intention and roles of the Master/student relationship. One of the most basic tenets of Light and Sound regarding the role of the Master is that the Master does not command, but merely suggests and "shows," as well as "tells." This principle has its roots in the great spiritual law of personal freedom. As soul, we all have the freedom to create our own attitudes, opinions, and ways of life, providing we do not infringe on another's right to do the same. It is a severe violation of this law to unduly influence another individual in any way. We must constantly respect this law of psychic space and allow others the freedom of their own choices and decisions. True Masters are always extremely sensitive to this great law in their relationships with their students. The Masters will suggest a certain course of action, a general way of life, or a spiritual discipline, but will never demand that any student follow their guidance.

The Master suggests, prods, and leads by example and, at the same time, demands that students take action and walk the path themselves. The Master in no way seeks to dominate the student, but neither will he allow himself to become a dispenser of spiritual welfare. His role is to guide and instruct his students regarding the great universal laws and how to come into harmony with them. In doing so, he allows the students the freedom to make their own decisions and mistakes; yet he is standing nearby to pick up the pieces and help the students regain their footing when they stumble and fall. The Master's love for the students is so great that he often sheds many tears as they fall victim to their own freedom of error and egotistical tendencies which prevent them from following the Master's guidance.

The Master's greatest role in assisting the student comes from the two faces of the Master. Any true Master of Light and Sound can assist the student both outwardly and inwardly. Many past masters and saints have roamed our planet spreading truth and the message of the Divine One; however, they are no longer present on earth in the physical body. Only a current living Master can present the two faces of the Master to the seeker; only he can manifest to the student both outwardly and inwardly. The outward or external assistance comes in the form of instruction, letters, discourses, phone calls, group discussions, personal meetings, etc. However, meeting the Master inwardly is entirely different.

When students learn to focus their attention at the third eye, they will discover the Inner Master is there waiting for them. Here, with the Inner Master, the student will find the highest and most sublime manifestation of truth ever encountered. It is one thing to talk to a Master and experience his presence outwardly, but meeting the Master in one's own inner Kingdom is by far more significant, for the inner form is unencumbered by the physical body and its limitations and can guide and direct the student in a more thorough and complete fashion. With the Inner Master, students can experience the many dimensions of consciousness and regions of the inner universes which lie beyond our physical perception; students can actually experience life after death while still living in the physical body.

You may know of people who have had such an experience through a vision, a near-death experience, astral projection, or some other method of parting one of the many veils separating the lower worlds from the higher. Hopefully these experiences were positive; many such adventures do not turn out so well. The traps and dangers of traveling the inner worlds unaided are numerous. Many who attempt the journey without expert guidance are damaged psychologically for life. Some have been unable to return to the physical body after astral projection; others have come under the control of highly negative entities who make their homes in the lower astral worlds. Perhaps these problems stem from our concepts of heavenly beauty and bliss; we have been taught to expect only beauty, light, and truth in the inner realms. This is just not true, especially on the astral plane, where there is almost as much negativity, violence, deceit, etc., as we find here in the physical world. For this reason of safety alone, a competent guide is absolutely necessary.

Traveling unaided on the inner planes can easily become a journey of delusion. Besides the obvious conflicts with negative entities, there also exists the enormous potential of being misled by the beauty and grandeur of some of the inner planes, where it is very easy to be overwhelmed by the partial levels of beauty, bliss, and truth available on the inner journey of soul.

As we expand in consciousness through regions of finer and finer vibration, each succeeding dimension is far more beautiful, more alluring, and more spiritual than the one preceding it. It is also coarser, less beautiful, and less spiritually charged than the next "higher" plane in the inner worlds. Some areas can be so alluring that we are certain we have found the source of all beauty, truth, and love; and many spiritual travelers or mystics have founded religions or metaphysical paths as a result of their journeys into the inner worlds. The danger here is that we can easily stop too soon. Each spiritual plane or region is only a reflection of the next. To travel through the many inner dimensions of experience with a true Master as a guide makes it highly unlikely that we will mistake the relative beauty of some lesser level of heaven for the greater levels of truth and spirituality which lie beyond. Thus, one should never attempt to travel the inner planes alone.

The greatest role of the outer or physical form of the Master is to introduce us to the inner form of the Master. The outer Master is restricted by time, space, and the limitations of the physical body, just as we are. The Inner Master, having no such restrictions, can work inwardly with one student or 100 at the same time, and can be contacted inwardly 24 hours a day. With no restrictions of time, space, or body, his inner form is with his students at all times.

The outer, living Master teaches the student to contact the inner form of the Master. He guides and instructs his students on how to focus their attention in the third-eye center. As a student regains the soul's energies that have been scattered out into the world and learns to still the mind enough to concentrate attention, the meeting with the Inner Master occurs. This is the great promise of Light and Sound—the living Master can give the student the key to meeting the Inner Master if the student so desires. The only condition that can possibly stop the student is a personal lack of sincerity or effort.

Once the student is able to experience the Radiant Form of the Inner Master, the job of the outer, living Master is basically finished. His role has been fulfilled, for now the Inner Master becomes a presence through which students begin to see into the heart of life. The students are constantly given love, guidance, and assistance from the Inner Master. Any time students place their attention on the Master, they are in communication with him. The Inner Master guides the student inwardly at all times via flashes, insights, intuitions, and even through dreams as the student sleeps. The bond that exists between the student and the Inner Master is like none other on earth.

CHAPTER 3

HUMAN CONSCIOUSNESS AND SPIRITUAL CONSCIOUSNESS

As we survey our own inner workings, and as we observe them in others, we see both vast differences and striking similarities in what captures our attention and what is energized by our feelings. The word *consciousness* denotes any level of awareness in which the seeker lives each moment. Consciousness exists on many varied levels of awareness. We give life and meaning to the many levels of consciousness that exist within our being through the soul's faculty of attention. Each of our five bodies has its particular concerns and interests as well as its particular ways of viewing these concerns.

The human state of consciousness is concerned with our first four bodies—the physical body and its needs; the astral body and its desires and feelings; the causal body with its karma and its propensity to be continually creating through thought, word, and deed; and the mental body where thought originates and we use reason to solve our problems. These four bodies, each with its own set of senses and concerns, make up the human state of consciousness.

When our attention is fused to the separate (yet simultaneous) activity of the first four bodies, we think, feel, behave, and live our lives within the confines of the human state of consciousness; within this basic division of reality we can see many different viewpoints. Some people appear to be kind, joyful, and content; others appear to feed on anger, fault-finding, and gossip. Some are motivated by sexual needs; others by creative artistic temperaments.

Each different point of view represents a level of awareness within the human state of consciousness. Some viewpoints center on the physical body and its needs; others on experiencing life through feelings and emotion; still others relate to mental qualities and their expressions. No matter how varied these levels of vibration may be, all are contained within the human state of consciousness. Our somewhat fulfilling, yet often entrapping human consciousness can indeed be compared to the cocoon, out of which the butterfly of soul will one day grow and rise above.

The Birth and Way of Human Consciousness

> *Kabir, what are you doing, always sleeping?*
> *Why don't you stand up and begin searching?*
> *The One from whom you are now so far away*
> *become united with again, so Kabir does say.*

Kabir
15th century Master of Light and Sound

> *Thou, O God, hast made us unto*
> *thyself, and the heart of man is*
> *ever restless, until he rests in Thee.*

Augustine
ca. 354 – 430
Catholic mystic

Long before humankind lived on this planet, soul existed. Soul was created out of the essence of God Itself in the image and likeness of its Creator. Questions often arise in the mind of the seeker: If soul were created in such divinity and purity, why is it necessary for it to enter into the human form and experience life in the physical worlds?

Why do the lower four bodies and planes (physical, astral, causal, mental) even exist? Why can't we, as soul, enjoy eternity with our Creator, basking in the God-essence of the soul body and living in the splendor of the higher heavens—the soul plane?

The Masters of Light and Sound often say that these questions are best asked at the latter stages of spiritual development when the soul body is highly activated and capable of a far greater and deeper understanding than the mind can produce. Some Masters even suggest these questions be saved until soul meets the Merciful One face-to-face and can ask the questions directly!

The point remains that soul is our original and true identity; the human body and the human consciousness came later. Soul needs a physical body to experience life in the physical worlds. This body corresponds to the vibration of the physical plane and protects soul from the coarser rate of vibration that exists in the physical worlds, just as we human beings need warmth and shelter from the storms of the physical worlds.

All earth forms, all space, and indeed, all atoms actually are soul. The Masters tell us that the entire universe and all the four "lower" planes are filled with souls. Many levels of awareness exist below human consciousness, and each soul moves through many levels of experience and states of consciousness to reach the human form. By the time soul is embodied in a human form, it is also endowed with the other four bodies. When soul evolves to such a state, human consciousness is born.

When soul reaches the human state of consciousness, it has the ability to recognize its true identity and to spiritualize its consciousness by taking the inner journey of self-remembrance. Just as the mighty oak is contained within the acorn, human consciousness provides the opportunity and the link to spiritual consciousness, which lies latent within the soul body.

It is human nature to seek an identity of some kind. If we cannot identify with our soul body and its unique viewpoint and concerns, we seek to identify with the mind, the emotions, the physical body, the ego, and the personality to define and give meaning to ourselves in some way. The choices we make at this juncture are crucial, for they become the key to unlocking the door that leads from the human state of consciousness into the spiritual. The single most limiting characteristic of the human state of consciousness is its attitude of being separate from the Creator. Our identification with our lower bodies leads us to believe that we are separate—not only from each other, but from the Divine as well—and becomes the earmark of the human state of consciousness.

Some of the finest human beings on Earth cannot fathom themselves as more than just decent, good people. These kind, sweet, loving people are still bound by the illusion of separateness from God and a lack of awareness of their divine nature and origin. They identify with the ego, the personality, and the mind so strongly that despite all their good deeds and genuine compassion, they fail to recognize their innate divinity. This lower self-centered viewpoint that characterizes the human state of consciousness is an outgrowth of the feeling of separateness that exists within the human consciousness.

The human state of consciousness operates in illusion—basically a state of unawareness—mistaking the appearances of reality for reality itself. In fact, the great Master Jesus stated that humanity appears to be asleep—even dead—within the human consciousness. If we entertain any notion of breaking this potent spell of illusion, we must further explore the makeup of the four lower planes of experience and the corresponding lower four bodies, for it is the lower bodies and their accompanying states of consciousness that now keep us entrapped.

The soul body is our true identity and the only faculty through which we can discern truth from falsity. Soul can instantly see, know, and be truth, but only when the mental, causal, astral, and physical bodies are brought into a state of balance and harmony.

The question remains: how have these lower bodies become unbalanced and been led to the perception of illusion rather than truth? The Masters teach that the Audible Life Stream, the Holy Spirit, emerges from the Creator to sustain all the worlds but does not remain a singular, unified stream of consciousness. After It passes through the soul plane, It divides into two great currents—the positive and negative streams—and all the lower four planes of creation are the result of the interplay and attraction of these two opposing currents. Therefore, the lower planes are the worlds of duality, and all things in the lower worlds exist in relation to their opposites. Can we have mountains with no valleys? Would the concept of up have any meaning if there were no down? Does male have any meaning apart from female? Does heat exist if we cannot relate it to cold? Can we separate the concept of matter from energy, or space from time? All ideas of reality exist in relation to their opposites—the result of the split in the Audible Life Stream that allows the dual worlds to exist.

This quality of duality exists in the subjective human consciousness as well. Can we know happiness without sadness? What does aggression mean without passivity, or love without hate? Life within the human consciousness continually vacillates between opposing external realities—night and day, hot and cold, rain and sunshine—as well as the opposing internal realities. One day we are content; the next day, restless. One moment we are happy; the next moment, sad. Today we act logically; tomorrow, irrationally. This continual shifting between polarities in the human state of consciousness relates back to the separation of consciousness from its own divine nature and identity, punctuated by fear—fear of not being loved or accepted, fear of losing our house or apartment, fear of the unknown or of others' opinions. Because all these fears are given birth within the human state of consciousness, when we recognize our innate oneness with the Creator, all our fears fall away.

In this human state of affairs, we seek to complete ourselves through the pursuit of happiness, good feelings, security, and the personal love of others, only to find that such seeking leads to temporary happiness and relative security and to good feelings suddenly turning sour. This dilemma of the human state of consciousness—seeking outside for that which can only be found within—is the web of illusion in which the human state of awareness is ensnared. We are like the stag wandering through the forest, following a scent, not realizing the musk is located within him.

The human state of consciousness values the dualities in the lower worlds. Defining these currents as positive and negative only relates to their opposing polarities; it does not judge them. The mind and emotions define the "good" or "bad" of these forces, thus judging almost everything we encounter. For instance, how often do we think of work as the lesser part of our lives and leisure as the better part? How many people see either men or women as the inherently superior gender and the other as inferior?

Soul, on the other hand, values all experiences for the spiritual lessons that are provided in them; it sees experiences as neither good nor bad, in and of themselves. Living meagerly is no worse than being wealthy from soul's point of view. While the mind and emotions certainly may have their strong opinions about it, soul stays serenely detached and balanced, viewing all situations in life as spiritual opportunities. This is not to say that it is wrong to attempt to escape poverty or to try to heal a sick body, it only means that soul's overview is far more inclusive than the mental and emotional outlook to which the human state of consciousness lends itself.

The key to understanding the human state of consciousness lies in recognizing it as a creation of the mind and emotions, based on a value system at a particular point in time in soul's journey. Human consciousness identifies the ego and the personality as reality to protect itself from harm as it seeks to deal with its painful separation from its Creator. Thus, it creates its own mini-identity, which thrives on pleasure and seeks to avoid anything it labels as pain.

The very nature of the human mind helps create and perpetuate the state of awareness in which the seeker lives daily. We live largely within the human consciousness on a day-to-day basis. This prevailing outlook is supported by the church, the educational system, and society in general. Previous lifetimes and their karmic creations and ensuing effects establish the primary conditions of each current lifetime. Heredity, early childhood training, environment, and education all play a role in shaping the human state of consciousness. By the time we reach the age of seven or eight, our defenses have hardened, our spiritual identification rests in deep slumber, and human consciousness rules.

We have been told that the mind is our most cherished possession and most powerful instrument, that its creative powers are nearly limitless, and that it has a tremendous capacity for reason and taking initiative. **The Masters of the Light and Sound do not agree!**

Contrary to psychologists' claims, the Masters teach that the human mind is much more like a machine; it is not original in thought and only reacts to stimuli or situations as it has been trained to do. It is soul, activated by the Audible Life Stream, that empowers the mind. Only when soul's forces are the motivating factor behind the mind can intelligence and rational action come to the fore. We can even observe the mind's reactive nature as it creates habitual patterns of response, which cause us to behave much more like machines or robots than enlightened spiritual beings. Would the world, our countries, and our communities be in the condition we observe if soul, through the action of the Holy Spirit, were in control?

All activity in our universe is carried on by the action of the Divine Spirit (the Sound Current); without Its life-sustaining impulses, everything would die. This spirit of God moves mind, and lends to it intelligence, wisdom, love, and the power to reason and remember. The mind loves its routines and, by itself, never varies from its conditioned responses to life. Its first reaction to any situation is a reaction that its past-life conditioning and early training demand, and it has established certain response patterns that it habitually falls back on in all similar situations. It enjoys its own habits and responses; it dislikes change and resists most attempts at innovation.

Giving all our vital energies to the concerns of the human state of consciousness allows the spiritual state within us to lie dormant. The spiritual energies of Light and Sound exist to reverse this condition of the mind, allowing for the divine, inward journey of soul. Without strong personal effort and the guiding grace of a true Master, the many potent illusions of the mind ensnare the brightest and most devoted seekers.

The Birth and Way of Spiritual Consciousness

> *Blessed is the person who always*
> *keeps his eye on the goal.*

> Rumi
> 13th century Muslim saint of Persia
> Master of Light and Sound

This valuable body you got
    after roaming in millions of lower lives.
Now do not lose it in vain pursuits.
Take heed! Give attention to your Devotion.

Swami Ji Maharaj
19th century Master of Light and Sound

Spiritual consciousness is one in which soul is awakened; it is a product of the energies and impulses of soul rather than the desires and opinions of the mind. Those who live in spiritual consciousness are generally seen as a breath of fresh air by those who live in the confines of the human state of consciousness. They radiate warmth, express their love by acting for the benefit of those with whom they come in contact, and appear joyous and content in life. But these people did not reach this state unaided. Nearly all spiritual seekers eventually gravitate toward a true Master, for without this pure help and expert guidance, the search is apt to be long and only relatively successful.

One interesting phenomenon that often confounds seekers is that of having been found by a true Master. Although even serious spiritual students often feel that it is we who can choose to accept or reject the Master, in fact, this is not the case when one is on the divine journey of soul. The Audible Life Stream, personified on the physical plane as a true Master, actually invites those who are ready for the journey. The unprepared cannot gain admittance, and nothing can stop the sincere seeker whom spirit selects for entry to the path.

This spiritual reality is often difficult to accept from the point of view of the human state of consciousness. We fancy ourselves to be quite independent and in control of our own destinies, when quite the reverse is true: the human state of consciousness is much more dependent than independent. We continually depend on each other's actions and emotional support to sustain our happiness and well-being. We depend on our pride and our self-esteem, and we rely on many external items and conditions to allow us to experience contentment. The idea that spirit abides, rules, and commands often offends our limited, human consciousness and its false sense of control and independence.

Seekers often experience difficulty with spirit's certainty. The mind asks: How can you be so sure of this truth? The human state of consciousness lends itself to uncertainty and lack of clarity and commitment, constantly hashing over opposite points of view, leaning toward one point of view one moment, then seeing more value in the opposite point of view the next. We tend to be indecisive and just can't seem to make up our minds, riding on an endless seesaw, viewing the polarities of a given situation, and experimenting with a temporary identification with each viewpoint. Soul, with its unique capacity for knowing and seeing truth, can easily see truth without argument or indecision. This causes a reaction in our minds when, through the designs of spirit, or perhaps via the Master, we are presented with a definitive point of truth.

The collision between the human and the spiritual states of consciousness provides the seeker with great opportunity. The student can decide either to ignore the higher truth being presented or to test the new recognition. For example, let's say that you're doing your laundry and watering the lawn, and you want to go to an afternoon matinee movie. School doesn't even start for another six weeks, yet suddenly you *know* that today is the deadline to sign up for classes at night school. You had not been giving the matter any thought, and really weren't at all aware that the deadline was today, or even this week. Yet suddenly you *just know*. It can be quite easy for the mind to jump in and begin arguing that this is just some silly fear and has no basis in fact. After all, it is six more weeks until school starts. You really want to relax this afternoon and go to the movies as planned, with extra butter on the popcorn. However, the certainty of your knowingness persists, so you go down to the school and discover that not only is today the last day to sign up for the class on Psychology of the Human Mind, but also there is only one more opening! Can you imagine the joyousness of life consistently lived on this level of truth and knowingness?

Spiritual consciousness is the awakening of soul, the state of awareness that lies beyond the mind, that all seekers yearn to experience. Awakening of soul means that soul is totally aware of its own existence, no longer encumbered by the various viewpoints of the four lower bodies and their incessant concerns and demands.

The seeker of truth becomes the knower of truth! In this superconscious state of awareness, we are now able to use soul's faculties of seeing and hearing for large portions of the day and to see truth and life consciously through soul's guidance. As the iron shackles which tie us to our karma and taint our viewpoints with fear and desire unlock, we can live in a spiritual state of consciousness characterized by beauty, contentment, true happiness independent of external conditions, freedom, and universal love for all.

The pursuit, discovery, and actualization of the spiritual state of consciousness is the primary purpose of all life. This spiritual awareness, the gift of the Divine to soul, lies dormant within each of us. The first, cardinal principle of Light and Sound is that soul exists because God loves it. God shows Its love for soul by bestowing on it all the divine attributes such as freedom, wisdom, love, power, and understanding. Soul's divine duty and joy is to display its love for the Creator by realizing that the gift exists, and then accepting and actuating the gift. The underlying purpose of life is not peace on earth, two cars in every garage, food and medicine for all, or the abolition of death of the physical body: it is to receive God's gift. Some of these worldly goals are noble and define the product of the finest human thought. Still, they all fall short of the goals and purpose that the Nameless One has set forth.

God's purpose and design is for soul to know its true inheritance. Just as we honor our teachers for their gift of knowledge by applying what they teach, through birthing the spiritual consciousness within soul, we can thank the Creator for the gift of life, or consciousness. Working more for greater comfort and happiness within the human state, while neglecting soul's inner journey to spiritual consciousness, is putting the cart before the horse. Real, genuine, lasting change is the product of the spiritual consciousness within us, not of the mind and its designs. As more and more souls come to discover their own true nature, and as the level of vibration of our world increases, we will see great changes. However, the human state of consciousness will never be responsible for any world society that matches the ideals of its highest aspirations.

To better understand spiritual consciousness, let's look more closely at our spiritual constitution. *Chakra*, a word from the Sanskrit language, means wheel. It refers to the spiritual centers within our five bodies, which serve to take in and distribute the spirit which surrounds us all. Just as we have organs within the body to perform certain physical functions, we also have these six invisible energy centers within the physical body which correspond to certain spiritual functions.

The first chakra is the rectal, or elimination center, at the base of the spine. It governs the process of elimination and, spiritually speaking, is the center of will power. Its lower aspect deals with understanding the more basic elements of life such as survival, and its higher aspect relates to birthing our will to spiritual liberation. Through this energy center, we experience the basic biological flight-or-fight reaction of all animals. Its physical counterpart is the adrenal gland.

The second chakra is located within the reproductive organs. It governs attitudes in relationships, sex, and reproduction, and is closely tied to creativity. Its external counterparts are the testes or ovaries. The third chakra, the navel or solar plexus chakra, is responsible for nourishment, including how we nourish ourselves in life through fame, honor, prestige, pride, etc. The higher aspect relates to how we nourish ourselves spiritually. This chakra is also tied to our emotional sensitivities and personal power struggles. Its external counterpart, the pancreas, governs the actions of the gall bladder, stomach, liver, and spleen.

The fourth chakra, the heart, is responsible for the circulation of the blood and for breathing. It externalizes as the thymus gland, influences the immune system, and is the center through which we feel emotional, conditional love or begin the birthing of spiritual, unconditional love. The fifth chakra, at the throat, deals largely with the metabolism and externalizes as the thyroid gland. Its center is tied to our expression and communication, and it is known by the Masters as the dream center in humans. The sixth chakra, located just behind the eyes, is the headquarters of the mind and the soul. All other centers within the body are controlled from this central location, which is associated with the pineal gland; through it we consider our mental and spiritual natures.

One additional chakra is the third eye, where the Masters of Light and Sound ask their students to center their attention. The third eye actually is located in the astral body at a point behind and between the two eyes.

We choose to give meaning and life to our various desires, loves, and feelings by lending them our soul energies so that they may live. Most spiritual seekers' states of awareness are located somewhere within the many levels of the human consciousness. Our energies are scattered throughout the chakras with much of our energies going out into the world. Lending our vital energies, our soul currents, to the chakras within the physical body energizes or vitalizes them. For example, those who are largely concerned with sexual conquest and feelings have centered their energies in the second chakra, which governs this type of thought and activity. Often, centering the attention here manifests as a great desire to have children. Those whose attention is largely given to nourishing themselves through attaining their goals in business, community, prestige, etc., make the third chakra the center of their attention. Many individuals whose primary concern is for the well-being of others and who have strong, genuine feelings about working for these goals center their attention primarily within the fourth chakra.

When we desire spiritual consciousness to grow and wish to reclaim rulership of our being from the grip of the human consciousness, soul must refocus its vitalizing spiritual energies. Giving life to the spiritual state of consciousness within us involves gathering up our divine energy from the lower chakras and bringing this energy up to the third-eye center, where true spiritual concerns and realities predominate. The knot which fastens the mind and soul together loosens as this chakra becomes activated, allowing soul to begin separating itself from the concerns of the mind and the emotions.

Soul's awakening does not require annihilating our personalities, zombifying our minds, or destroying our emotions. We have discussed how the Audible Life Stream splits Itself into positive and negative currents to create dual forms (male and female, night and day, etc.) to make possible life as we know it. We saw that these polarities, having been created by the split in the Holy Spirit, exist internally as well as externally. All states of emotion and qualities of thought have two sides to them as well. For instance, when the spiritual journey is undertaken, the energies begin rising within the body, coming from the first chakra that deals with our will or will power. In human consciousness, this personal will is characterized by determination to serve the ego, the mind, and the personality. Its opposite is the spiritual will, which becomes our will to liberation.

It is very important for spiritual seekers to have a strong will and desire for liberation to motivate us to continue on the journey of soul. Without a strong will or desire for liberation, we will find it too difficult and painful to confront our own lower self. So willpower is not annihilated; it is transmuted into a spiritual faculty that now works for the whole individual rather than seeking only to protect, enlarge, and propel the ego. The same principle applies to all of our emotional and mental faculties. When personal love (always dependent on certain conditions: Is *my* love returned? Are *my* needs being met?) is transmuted into unconditional, universal love, it is still love, just transformed. Love is not destroyed, only brought to a higher level of reality and manifestation. Logic is certainly not left behind but becomes our great ally in gathering and employing knowledge which will serve us not only in our worldly life, but in our spiritual pursuits as well.

All our inborn faculties of thought and emotion can serve us, or enslave us if they are not brought under control in the spiritual sense. All are extremely valuable. In birthing the spiritual state of consciousness, we turn the actions of the lower bodies around and get them working for soul and its concerns. One area that often concerns seekers is sexual desire. "Will it disappear and leave me celibate?" No. If we are out of balance regarding our sexual urges, we may find that we become more balanced regarding sex as the soul energies begin rising up the spine to the third-eye center. The natural urge remains, but in a less urgent and conditional way as it becomes transmuted into a desire for union with the Divine within us. No energies are lost.

Energy cannot be destroyed, only transmuted into a higher form of divine energy for our own betterment. Soul exists because God loves it. This is the heart of both the birth and the way of the spiritual consciousness.

From the Human to the Spiritual State of Consciousness

I think, therefore I am.

René Descartes
1596 – 1650
French philosopher, scientist, mathematician

Regions and universes, subtle planes and
*   nether worlds are created by the Nam [Spirit].*
It giveth life and form to all.

Guru Arjan Dev
16th century Sikh guru and
Master of Light and Sound

Descartes' statement is the perfect description of the human state of consciousness. The Masters of Light and Sound would reverse such a statement to "I am soul, therefore I know."

At some point on its sojourn into the lower worlds, after it has lived in countless bodies and forms and has experienced life in many ways, separate from itself and from the Divine, soul begins to catch a glimpse of its true self. Continually evolving through trial and error, pleasure and pain, soul reaches a point where it begins to recognize that merely experiencing the lower worlds and its lower bodies cannot fulfill its inborn yearning for union with the source of all goodness and truth. Because the human state of consciousness is one in which soul slumbers, our minds and emotions are our guiding lights; the pleasure of the senses of the lower four bodies dominates our attention. In this state our energies are dispersed among the chakras of the physical body, and our higher spiritual centers are dormant. Of what possible value can this state of affairs be?

The power of expression and experience given to us as soul in a human body is indeed enormous—we can experience life from endless points of view or attitudes, all within a given day. All experiences are of immense value to soul as it views the world through the human state of consciousness, aiding its spiritual journey, the journey of self-remembrance. Seeing and living life from the viewpoints of a beggar, doctor, housewife, or laborer allow soul to experience a particular part of the wholeness of itself. Each experience provides soul with the unique opportunity to relate to itself and the Divine in a different way and from a different level of awareness.

All experiences present us with tremendous learning opportunities to discover the true self that lies within each of us. Through eons of time, soul experiences life in many forms and many bodies, constantly creating, extending its energies of thought and emotions. Soul, separate from its Creator, has entered into its own period of self-regulation. Through accruing karma, both positive and negative, soul continues to experience the effects of its past incarnations, while laying the groundwork for and building its future identities and experiences by its present action.

Because soul exists in the lower worlds to experience life so that it can come to know itself, it must come to know what it is not. Thus, as we view soul's journey, we can see that many, many experiences and lifetimes spent with the human state of consciousness in control, seeking out millions of ways to define ourselves and to create an identity, are necessary to lead soul to its own awakening. How we see ourselves—as honorable, vain, guilt-ridden, happy, dull, or thoughtful—separates us from our true nature as soul because we define ourselves from these points of view of mind and emotions. Then we accept these self-created identities as truth and view ourselves and the world through this fabricated lens.

The wonder and the value of these self-created illusions reflect part of the Law of Spirit which states that future conditions always manifest out of the present; seeing ourselves through any particular point of view of mind or soul creates conditions which correlate directly with what we choose to see. In short, we create our own reality. This is certainly neither shocking nor new to any seeker. Yet how many of us are aware of its vast ramifications?

It is the nature of humans to desire. Soul must experience all the many ways in which human consciousness seeks love, intellectual stimulation, money and possessions, raising children, and a million other things. All are important, and all life experience has enormous spiritual value. We are always engaged in the process of wanting something, and we seek to fulfill the objects of our desires. All bodies (physical, astral, causal, mental, and soul) have their wish to merge with the objects of their desires as their agenda.

Desire motivates human consciousness and spiritual consciousness as well. Remember when you wanted to get your first driver license, and all your thoughts, emotions, and energy of will were aimed at fulfilling that one desire? Remember how all your feelings, thoughts, and behaviors constantly revolved around your first love? Desires come in many packages—some weak and others very strong.

Our families, mates, friends, jobs—**everything**—gives us exactly what we have asked for at every moment. What more perfect universe could we desire? This spiritual fact provides enormous value and meaning to soul in any state of consciousness. Within the human consciousness, we experience life just as we have created it, at any point, at any given moment. It is very helpful to understand that this is the key to freedom as well as the lock which imprisons us. We simply choose how we want to live by using our divine energies of thought and emotion. Then the world acts as a giant piece of modeling clay, receiving and imprinting our energies on itself. This allows us to experience the fruits of our own creations, and to become aware of the nature of our imprisonment, the confinement of our cell, and the folly of more prison reform, or more privileges, before we decide to break out of jail.

If within either the human or spiritual state of consciousness, we do not like what we are experiencing in life, externally or internally, we have the power to change it. How many of us take advantage of this wonderful gift of the Divine? Can we experience happiness, anger, lust, contentment, or any attitude simply by enlivening it with our energy of thought and emotion? Of course! We can do it right now. Do we have to wait to experience joy? If you truly desire to, can't you be joyful right now?

Soul has tried to discern truth through mind alone and to experience joy through the senses of the lower bodies; still it remains unfulfilled. We certainly cannot say that soul's experiences in life are in vain or that they lack value or meaning. All were laden with value and meaning. All were relevant and necessary to bring soul to its current position of desiring a more meaningful life. When soul begins to rise from its slumber, the mind and emotions can no longer control it; as soul's wishes and desires come to the fore, it enters into conscious evolution. Now the truth seeker will consciously use soul's desire for spiritual liberation and truth as active substitutes for the karma-producing desires of the mind and emotions and consciously and willfully allow soul to out-create the lower bodies in thought, word, and deed.

Soul's grand desire is to merge with its Creator. It has been seeking to do so since it became separated from its home and entered the worlds of matter, energy, space, and time. Our architecture, music, literature, art, religions, and philosophy are all part of our attempts to find, define, and externalize the God with which soul so desperately seeks to merge. Thus the question for the spiritual seeker becomes, "Just what desires do I really want to fulfill?"

Until an individual actually becomes a truth seeker, the question of which desires to fulfill really has no relevance. The individual will go on seeking to fulfill all the desires of the lower four bodies, trying to find some sort of happiness while doing so. However, true seekers become aware of soul's desires as well. We may not yet be able to live within the spiritual state of consciousness, but we are aware soul exists and feel its divine impulses calling us to find it, realize it, and actualize it. Truth seekers are in the unique position of being beckoned by the human level of awareness to fulfill its desires, as well as by the latent spiritual state of consciousness, which seeks to merge with soul and the divine traits within.

We need to make a choice. Is the will to liberation stronger than the desires of the mind? If we choose to pursue spiritual truth and the inner journey of soul, our lives will change drastically. As serious students begin to raise their energies up toward the third eye, a new outlook on life is born. We discover a contentment and a joy within that heretofore evaded us. Nagging problems, insecurities, anger, fears, and overly emotional reactions begin to disappear. Over time, the spiritual state of consciousness becomes less and less a dream or a fantasy and more and more an attainable goal and a spiritual reality. The meaning of consciousness is growth; the unfoldment of soul is of divine origin and purpose.

The choice is always our own, and is always present.

CHAPTER 4

THE MASTER —
HUMAN IDEAS AND SPIRITUAL REALITY

Humankind has existed for several million years, and approximately six billion people now populate the earth. If we counted all the years of human existence and multiplied this by the number of humans who are or have ever been on earth, the result would boggle the mind. But for all these years of human life on earth, what do we know of our physical world? How far have we really progressed in science, technology, or medicine? Whatever your answer might be, we can agree that it will probably take trillions more human years just to unlock all the secrets of the physical universe. Merely understanding our physical makeup and surroundings pales in comparison to understanding our other four bodies and their corresponding planes of activities. We have vast universes within us of which we know little or nothing at all.

To many seekers, the idea of attaining levels of consciousness and realization that exist within the soul are only fanciful dreams. Others feel they can attain self-realization and God realization alone. They honestly believe that in just one human lifetime, they can come to understand their physical, astral, causal, and mental bodies, and reach the soul level of consciousness through their own efforts in about seventy-five years, alone and unaided.

When we compare the feat of attaining God realization to the task of understanding the physical world, there is really no comparison, especially when an astronomical number of human years has so far left us unable even to master the physical worlds! We must find a true Master to lead us to self-realization and God realization—we will never be able to find our way alone. The journey is far too vast, too complex, and too laden with detours and dead ends for even the most sincere seekers to complete without the aid of a true Master. But how can one more human and another seventy-five years make the odds so much better for the seeker? Well, it certainly wouldn't if the Master were just one more human being. This, of course, is not the case. This is no mere human being who comes to aid us. A true Master is one with life itself—one who has resolved the haunting question of separation from the Creator and has reunited with all of God's qualities of wisdom, freedom, power, and love. The Master brings the power of the universe to the equation—not only our universe, but all universes in all dimensions of experience.

No doubt the soul within us desires to be reunited with the Divine; soul wants to go home. There also is no doubt that the ego and the mind want to stay right where they are—in control. Thus, the battle lines are drawn, and victory for seekers depends much more on the nature of our ally than on the quality of our troops. We may be well armed with a keen mind, a strong desire for truth, and a powerful will to liberate ourselves from the clutches of illusion, but it is our ally, the Master, who allows us to snatch victory from the jaws of defeat. The Master is no mere teacher or sage; in his arsenal he carries and delivers the power to transform. The Master is life; he knows the highest truth and imbues his students with the power of awareness to bring truth to form, thereby empowering us to live soul's path.

The Human Perception of the Master

> *The counterfeit coin and the genuine,*
> *both, O Lord, have been made by you,*
> *and you yourself are the judge.*
> *The coins that are genuine*
> *you put in your treasury;*
> *The base ones are rejected and left to wander,*
> *Lost in delusion.*

Guru Amar Das
16th century Sikh guru

The Master is available only to those who make room for him or her. If we see God as true reality and ourselves as prisoners of the human consciousness and the world, then we will believe only death can unite these two separate realities. This common misconception creates a gap between us and God that disallows the idea that a Master can even exist, for if we view human consciousness as a barrier rather than a gateway to the God within, then the Master has no route to reach us.

As we begin the inner journey of self-discovery and remembrance, it becomes apparent that a wealth of God-like qualities lie dormant within us. Untapped reservoirs of divine love for all life, the ability to see things for what they truly are, and the power to actuate the spiritual consciousness are all perceived as real by the sincere seeker. This incipient awakening to our divine potential allows us to begin to accept the idea that perhaps others have been able to fully release and activate that same potential within themselves and have become the masters of their own consciousness.

When one Master of Light and Sound was asked, "How does one become a Master?" she replied, "Simply let him out!" The nature of our minds separates humankind from other life forms on our planet. But when the mind and ego claim rulership of our being, then they also separate us from soul and God. The Master comes to us only when we truly want him. The Master exists in a state of unity with the God within, and our sincere desire to unite ourselves with our true nature is an expression of our need for him. As we awaken to our deep desire to experience the beauty of spiritual consciousness within us, we consciously and unconsciously draw the Master closer and closer to us, allowing in time for a meeting with him.

Those in the human state of awareness sometimes see the outer Master as a supreme egotist because he rarely denies that he is the Master. Thus, he is judged as being egotistical and lacking humility. This human reaction to the Master is rooted in the mind and the ego, which hate to admit that another individual is superior. Our minds may react against the Master because we do not yet recognize our own true nature. The unenlightened feel that the Master is pompous, arrogant, and even a fool for proclaiming his own divinity. The self-critical see themselves as a separate ego, perhaps created by God, but certainly not God-like. They know their own shortcomings very well as they easily become angry, lustful, vain, and full of desires and self-serving attitudes; with their obvious limitations they can't imagine another mortal claiming to be more than they are, so they attack the Master for lacking humility.

However, these critics have confused humility with modesty. The Master is not a modest man. It is his duty and mission to tell those who come to him who he is in no uncertain terms. Anything less than this is a disservice to the true seeker who needs him, and a case of false modesty as well. Still, the Master is a living, breathing example of humility at all times. He constantly points to his divinity, not as a product of the mind and ego, but as a union with the God within us all. He always gives credit to the Creator for the transformations he apparently brings about in his students. He never boasts of his accomplishments as being done by a personality. In fact, he is often self-deprecating in his humor and points always to the Inner Master as being the true Master. In *The Call for the Master*, Dürckheim states: "To be truly humble is not just to avoid seeming more than one is—it is also to accept that one is, in some respects, more than one seems."

Language has many limitations, and misperceptions based on our everyday use of language abound. The word *master* is used simply because the Master is the ruler of his own consciousness. Reunited with his own true nature—soul—he has discovered and unleashed the Divine within. The Master controls the mind and emotions from the elevated level of the true self, while the student is still seeking to do so. The very word, *master,* has connotations in our language that can easily lead the seeker astray. We often associate the word *master* with the word *slave*. In a master/slave relationship, one party has all the power, controls the other through fear, and consumes the energy of the other party for one's own personal gain. The slave is denied basic freedoms and individuality and is constantly manipulated by the master. This abusive, debasing relationship is the product of some of the worst motives and thoughts of the human consciousness.

The Master/student relationship has no resemblance whatsoever to a master/slave relationship.

The Master does not command but only suggests a spiritual course of action to the students. The students are free to live life as they wish—their individuality is highly respected and encouraged, and everything the Master does is for their benefit. Another popular misconception is that the Master/student relationship resembles the master/pet relationship. A pet is dependent on its master for food, water, shelter, love, affection, and protection. The student in the Master/student relationship discussed here bears no resemblance to a pet. The Master teaches that we should be self-supporting and as independent as possible. He also stresses that rather than showering the Master with our personal love, we should give it to our friends, family, and most of all to ourselves. The Master teaches unconditional love for all life, and love, sensitivity, and respect for ourselves as spiritual beings who have been created from the fabric of God.

These common misconceptions about the word, *master*, also show us that we often view the Master and his work as a predominately external phenomenon. When the Master is seen as merely another human being, apart from us, then all our fears and suspicions about a master may surface, enlivening grave concerns about losing one's individuality, being manipulated, and being cast into the slave or pet role. Be ever aware that knowing the Master is primarily an *internal,* not an external, experience. His way of bringing about change within us is geared to our inner workings and not to our external lives. The Master does not seek to control our way of life, but to transform us by teaching how to enlarge our points of view. To this end he works ceaselessly through the inner channels, providing us with situations, experiences, dreams, revelations, and insights which lead us to broaden our viewpoints.

The human perception of the Master is that our minds are being taught by the outer, physical Master. Actually, soul is the true disciple, and the Inner Master (the personification of the Audible Life Stream) is the true guru. These two divergent points of view lie at the crux of the issue of the human perception versus the spiritual reality of the Master. When we are able to transcend the human idea and come to see the spiritual reality, then the master/slave or master/pet issues become irrelevant. We then see and know that the Master's intention is not to control our behavior, and that he has no desire to be the object of our worship. Then the whole concept of "following a Master" radically changes, and we come to understand that our obedience to the Master is an internal affair which involves opening ourselves up to the opportunities for spiritual growth that the Master presents.

The mysterious workings of the true Master—the Inner Master— provide the true student—the soul—with all that is necessary to first attain self-realization, and then God realization. The duty of the outer Master is to bring us to where we can see and allow the Inner Master within each of us to be released. Thus, following an outer Master becomes a process of meeting, greeting, and recognizing the slumbering Inner Master that lies within us all.

If we see the outer Master as just another ego, then we assume that his concerns are somewhat similar to our own—concerns about the physical problems of life. If we expect the Master to act in our behalf as a cupid; as a finder of lost articles; or as a benefactor who brings us a fine, new home, a better job, or more money, we bring the Master down from his spiritual plateau to the physical level of our mundane concerns. In this way we totally misconstrue and misunderstand his true purpose and mission—to bestow love and transform consciousness.

The human idea of the Master demands unearned relief from our self-created karma. The Master isn't here to alter the situations of our physical lives, to perform miracles, or to dole out spiritual welfare. We have all created our own life situations, and we ourselves must deal with what we have created. The Master provides the correct viewpoint on our karma and day-to-day life; and with his spiritual strength and insight, which are ours for the asking, we learn to transcend conditions that may be bothersome now and avoid creating similar situations in the future. We expect relief, but the Master offers understanding and guidance—far greater gifts than we may believe them to be.

It is much like the story of the man who was starving in his little shack by the sea, while his neighbor, a mile or two away, was quite healthy and vibrant. When the neighbor came by one day, the hungry man swallowed his pride and asked, "Please, do you have some fish I can have? I'm starving." The neighbor smiled and said, "Yes, of course, and after you eat, perhaps I can teach you how to fish." The human idea of the Master asks for fish to feed us; the spiritual reality of the Master offers to teach us how to fish.

By instilling in us the spiritual values of right thinking, the ability to control our attention, and a sense of serene spiritual detachment, the Master gently opens our spiritual eyes so that reality can be directly perceived. As the web of illusion gives way to love and truth, the sincere seeker becomes the spiritualized being. Soul is on the ascendant now, and the ability to see and create life from its divine viewpoint replaces the usual endless quest for happiness within the confines of the human state of awareness. Understanding and love are the twin traits of the Divine and are Its gifts to the "whole" person.

The basic dilemma of the human idea of the Master is that it expects the Master to deal with our separate parts rather than the whole. This relates to how we see ourselves as separate from God and each other. Because the Master is the ultimate holistic healer, always working from the overview of the whole rather than the limited points of view of the parts, he seeks to teach us how to fish rather than just being a cosmic fishmonger. Human consciousness desires a cure for its external ills, but the Master's remedy for all our cares is to treat the source of all our maladies—our separation from soul. His prescription provides a true healing rather than a temporary fix for our symptoms.

The Spiritual Reality of the Outer Master

Marked by and charged with this greater Life, guided by and serv-ing it, the master has matured to a point where he can manifest the Absolute. He has overcome many of the obstacles that prevent Life from emerging fully, and is thus human and superhuman at the same time.

K. G. Dürckheim
1896 – 1988
German psychologist, author, philosopher

The teachings of the Masters of Light and Sound tell us that we must locate a true, outer Master—the link between God and human —to experience spiritual liberation. This has been true since time began, and will always be so. While he lives in the world, he is known, as Jesus said, as the "Light of the World." A true Master is needed so that we can receive expert guidance and advice: "No man comes to my Father but through me." Only one who is completely familiar with the many levels of consciousness and the spiritual regions within our universal bodies can lead us to our highest spiri-tual goals and aspirations. The Master's bond with us lasts until each one of us becomes the master of our own consciousness. Not even death can separate the Master from the student. The Master/ student relationship is the holiest and most significant relationship in all the universes, and one not to be entered into lightly.

The Master actually does very little in our lives. His mere pres-ence in our consciousness acts as a channel for the Audible Life Stream, which works through him and brings about profound change in those around him. Our minds must be convinced of the Master's authenticity before we can receive his greatest contribu-tions. Knowing all too well how the mind resists anything that claims to be greater than itself, the Master asks us not to surrender to him unconditionally, but to take our time and to experiment, allowing trust to grow naturally. He carefully and methodically allows us to experience his gifts and discover his true purposes and ideals. The Master comes not to support our illusions but rather to help us outgrow them. He uses the sword as well as the olive branch and the dove, as he overturns our neat, convenient, well-ordered delusions. We soon come to see that a new and greater reality has replaced the illusions of our previous, tightly held opinions and desires.

The Master intimately knows not only us, but the inner pathway as well. His strong arm guides us with gentleness and firmness; he knows what is holding each of us back. He is fully aware of the conditions which need to be born within us, as well as those that entrap us, and guides us through the various levels of the path, step by step, leading us to discover our own true inner natures. He knows when to lead and when to allow us our turn at the wheel; he is familiar with the signs that indicate progress as well as the many detours and dead ends. He guides the dying we all must do to experience the birth of greater life.

In a figurative sense, the Master may multiply the "loaves and fishes" within our lives; may allow us to become completely satiated within our own worldly desires; or may take every last morsel of meat and crumb of bread away. Both courses of action are done in love and for our betterment in accordance with our karmic debts. Both will allow us to see the correct value of our lives and help bring our desires into balance. When we properly negotiate these debts, we return to divine consciousness, which allows us to live in accordance with soul's will.

The Master lives much like the rest of us. Not seeking to distinguish himself in any ostentatious way, he assumes no special dress and lives modestly. The Master almost never asks anything of anyone, but is always the supreme giver. He rarely even accepts a gift unless the student's need to give is greater than the actual gift. He always instructs his students that the most elevated way they can express their love and appreciation for him is by truly seeing themselves as soul and by living in that light.

The Master uses no crystals, tarot decks, or horoscopes in his work. The only sacred gems he recognizes are those that adorn the crown of God realization: wisdom, love, understanding, truth, power, and freedom. He has no need for founding any new religion, but teaches that the pathway back to God, designed by the Creator, lies already complete within each of us. The Master has little concern for being recognized as who he really is. He knows that those souls who truly want his help and need him will come to know him. Therefore, he has no need to perform public miracles or prophesy openly to the world. Occasionally, he may reveal parts of the future privately to his students to allow them to see their divinity in a new, dramatic way.

The outer Master and the student have much in common in their divine bond. They both serve the same Inner Master. The Master always points to the Divine as his source of truth, and the student seeks only to accomplish the same goal. The Master and the student share the divine warmth which issues forth from the contact of one soul to another. Master and student also glow in the same light—that light which illuminates all conditions and circumstances as opportunities for spiritual growth and unfoldment.

The true Master knows our divine nature, and all that he does is to awaken us to our own inheritance; he has no other purpose, goal, or ulterior motive. He needs no churches, ashrams, or temples; he asks only that we be sincere and willing to be taught. Much more than a teacher or a sage, the Master exists to transform our raw iron into spiritual steel and to transmute our impure brass into shining gold—miracles that no mere teacher can ever accomplish. The student and the Master are two sides of the same coin, inextricably linked together in the loving process of unfoldment and self-discovery.

The most stunning display of a true Master's authenticity is his personal example of not only a commitment to truth, but the ability to actually *be* truth. A true Master sees past the defenses of the mind and ego, and into the very heart of our being; and addresses us with both total love and total understanding simultaneously. His ability to be a shining example of truth and the clarity that truth brings provides a bittersweet nectar for the thirsty seeker, but the Master never destroys without rebuilding, and never exposes poisons without providing the antidote. He actualizes the divine traits of love and wisdom as a magnet to draw out the negativity within us—the negativity that separates us from the God within and, at the same time, he refills our cups with greater spiritual values, desires, and realizations.

Unless the Master's teachings seem reasonable and possible, they are likely to fall on deaf ears—and well they should. Our spiritual search for truth should be based on personal experience and provide knowledge that is acceptable to the logical mind. The Master's task is to explain specific elements and situations to us and to show us how they relate to the great spiritual principles with which we must come into harmony in order to continue our spiritual growth. The Master does have a systematic, logical, step-by-step procedure to arrive at the God within, as all saints of all times have followed. He sees and knows truth as it has been laid out by the Divine.

The process remains intact, but each student experiences it in an individual, uniquely tailored fashion suited for him or her alone. The Master fully supports these differences because he completely understands that each of us is indeed the Way. The Master has no dogma. Each student's path is unique, and herein lies the difference between the Master's teachings (doctrine) and dogma, which states that everyone must approach truth in the same fashion and follow the same moral guidelines: pray alike, read the same scriptures, and fast on the same days. It is very important that a seeker understand this distinction. The Masters have rarely had any part in these rituals. The Masters of Light and Sound impose no dogma or moral code of any kind; rather, they allow personal experience (in harmony with truth) to lead us to correct thought, word, and deed.

Many who pass themselves off as masters today have not even transcended human consciousness. Seekers must be extremely cautious in casting their lots with any master until they have done some investigation. Perhaps the finest guideline is from Jesus: "By their fruits you shall know them." We as seekers must judge a master by his wares. A guru who promotes doctrine and guidelines that are less truthful and pure than those outlined here may fit into the category or phenomenon of the pseudo-guru.

Some external behaviors may help identify false masters. Pseudo-gurus use manipulation, fear, and pressure tactics. Upon meeting such an individual or his representative, seekers are often told that they need to decide to join immediately, or they may not get a second chance. They are asked to join an organization, often at great cost, without being given proper time to examine the issues and do some spiritual research and experimentation. Some pseudo-gurus have highly developed psychic senses and use them to read the minds of the seekers or to predict their futures—solely to impress seekers with their powers. A true Master never stoops to such levels of manipulation.

Many pseudo-gurus of our day demand exorbitant amounts of money or the release of property in trade for their blessings. A true Master never does. The pseudo-guru often says his blessings are so great that a gift to him must be equally as large in order to show sincerity and appreciation. A true Master, although he may ask a minimal fee to support his work, knows that the gifts of our attention and our desire for spiritual liberation show our sincerity and appreciation. These intangible gifts are all the Master requests.

Other false gurus shower their personal love upon the seeker and ask for all of the seeker's personal love in return, even asking their members to engage in sex with each other and with the guru. Sometimes the students are told that such behavior is meant to release their deep-seated karma and to overcome their emotional blockages. A true Master of Light and Sound does not engage in such practices. He may show affection for us, but his gifts are directed at our soul bodies, not our physical and emotional bodies.

Using sexual practices to gain spiritual enlightenment is an old and worldwide practice which involves centering one's unharnessed attention on the reproductive chakra and exciting it to the point of releasing unguided kundalini energy. When this powerful force travels up the spine to the third-eye chakra, the spiritual eye of the practitioner is opened. The kundalini energy is a powerful and dangerous force, and many times its premature release can cause insanity and even death. The Masters of Light and Sound teach that we should work on both centering and purifying our attention at the third eye, gently raising the soul currents through the body under a Master's expert guidance.

Many times, having the third eye opened by one who has not attained God realization is much like taking powerful psychedelic drugs. Users may experience highly increased spiritual awareness and sometimes even the accompanying powers, but after the experience wears off, they are right back where they started. If the third eye is opened prematurely by a false master, most students cannot keep it open. They return to where their energies are centered within the lower chakras, with no gain to show for their experience at all, except a fleeting vision.

No guru can raise a student above the guru's own level of consciousness. Most pseudo-gurus have their energies raised only to the navel or heart chakra; a few may have reached the third-eye center, which lies in the astral region. A true Master has attained God realization, a level of awareness located several major levels beyond the third-eye. A pseudo-guru who has reached the third-eye center may have strong psychic powers and awareness, which often impress a naive seeker. Such gurus often claim that they can open the third eye immediately—and they can. However, without proper spiritual preparation for this great event in the spiritual life, the seeker may encounter some very negative forces in the third-eye region with no idea how to control them, and may be overwhelmed by psychological damage, messianic visions, and even demonic possession.

The method of a true Master, who has attained union with the God within, is completely different, and so are the results. A true Master brings his students slowly and carefully through all levels of consciousness within their own beings without upsetting the delicate balance of their physical, emotional, and mental bodies. Realizing that the third-eye center is really just the beginning of the spiritual journey, not an end point, his methods result in permanent changes within the consciousness and spiritual life of his students. The Master possesses great power, the authority of the Divine to use it, and the wisdom and spiritual maturity to guide his students safely beyond their highest aspirations. These aspirations are really only dreams to the students because they do not know them. But the Master does. The pseudo-guru may claim and even display great knowledge, but has no proper authority. The true Master is commissioned by the Divine Itself, on whose command he acts, and to whom he is responsible.

The Spiritual Reality of the Inner Master

Seek the true Master with faith, love, and patience.
He will give the Light to find the hidden entrance.
If with constant effort you attune the Inner Ear,
The way to God opens and the Path will be clear.

Tulsi Sahib
19th century author, and Master of Light and Sound

If the mind cannot understand something, it usually discards that knowledge, so the Inner Master provides it in a way that is natural and conveniently supersedes the mind's propensity to negate whatever it doesn't understand.

Sri Gary Olsen
1948 –
Author and Master of Light and Sound

Jesus referred to the outer, living Master as "The Word made flesh." The outer Master is much more than a wise human being; he is ordained, not by bishops or cardinals, but by the Divine. This Master's job is to activate the Sound Current in all who come to him. Because soul is trapped within the human level of awareness, we barely even begin to contact the rarified levels of consciousness that lie within our own being. Becoming truly aware of ourselves as soul leads to self-realization. Actualizing this awareness in our lives leads to the Source within us from which all our five bodies are created and sustained—the Word, the essence of God, the Holy Spirit, or what is known as the Audible Life Stream, or Sound Current.

As the Master initiates us into this great stream of consciousness and increased awareness, all our perceptions change. We begin to see all life more from the overview than from our limited points of view. We feel and think differently; a greater desire for truth and the spiritual realities of existence replaces and enhances our goals in life. Our consciousness swiftly becomes spiritualized to a much greater degree, and the inner journey of soul immediately takes on new meaning and clarity.

The outer, living Master is the Word made flesh; the Inner Master is the Sound personified. The outer Master is limited by his physical body. He writes books and delivers seminars, but outwardly he is still only one individual. His method of connecting us directly with the Sound Current does not involve physical touching or union; it is done through the inner form of the Master. The Sound is everywhere, occupying every atom of space on all five planes (physical, astral, causal, mental, soul). There is nowhere where the Sound is not. The Audible Life Stream can transform Its formlessness and serve, guide, and direct all Its followers at any given moment of time. While the outer Master can only be in one place at one time, just like the rest of us, the Inner Master knows no such limitation and can be all places at one time. For a student of a true Master of Light and Sound, the Inner Master becomes one's constant guide and companion. Although it may take some time before we are able to see the Master inwardly, it takes no time for the Inner Master to begin to act. Once the inner form of the Master has stationed Itself within our auras, we become a terminal for the divine blessings of the Audible Life Stream. Our spiritual lives take on new colors and our horizons expand, often quite dramatically.

Both the outer and the Inner Master speak to soul. The only difference is that the outer Master must do so through the physical channels, while the Inner Master acts through the inner channels we make available to him. The Master, in both the inner and outer forms, brings us new life and truth. Simultaneously, a part of our old way of life must be transmuted, changed, or even left behind to make way for the new. The Master's spiritual gifts bring real meaning to many apparently meaningless experiences in our lives and lend perspective and understanding to an absurd world. They bring security and new understanding to us, even in the midst of our feelings of separateness and aloneness. Anger, fear, and even terror occasionally might seem appropriate reactions when the Inner Master is at work within us; instead, we find ourselves filled with divine joy and confidence. When we feel driven to despondency or despair, a new reality often uplifts us. Just when we feel lonely and forlorn, we suddenly experience the knowingness that we are loved and cherished.

The Inner Master dares us to accept what we feel unable to face alone, and to probe the limits and confines of the ego through a deepening personal honesty. As this process continues, the ego begins to collapse from its own weight, and soul shines more brightly. These experiences give birth to true inner awareness that transcends our thoughts, ideas, and emotional states. We find ourselves basking in strength—in the midst of our weaknesses. We view everything with greater clarity, even though those who surround us do not. And we experience the Master's love for us, while neither the world nor our own minds seem to care much for us.

The Inner Master is the Divine in action, not some formless, unreachable deity to which we cannot relate. Being Light and Sound Itself, the Inner Master is our true nature and our true self—the consciousness within us that all true seekers desire to find and to be. The Inner Master becomes our best friend as well as our highest goal. Once we experience being connected to the Sound Current, the life force, we are never happy apart from It.

The outer and inner forms of the Master are part and parcel of the same spiritual reality. It is our mind that conspires to see the One as two, just as it refuses to accept the fact that it needs help. Yet the outer Master is truly present for the taking. He promises to introduce us to the Inner Master and connect us in a way that we have never before experienced. He further states that the Inner Master, although It personifies Itself in the image of the outer Master, is actually our own true self. He offers his own inner form as a conduit to the Divine within us all, simply because soul is trapped within the human consciousness, and the Nameless One, in Its love, wishes to see soul return home.

The conflict between the human idea of the Master and the spiritual reality of the Master is reduced to the age-old battle of mind and soul. The Divine has always sent Its own to lead soul home. Soul sees and understands this well; however, mind rules the physical worlds, and soul is trapped in mind's illusion. The mind is extremely powerful in our world, much more so than the slumbering soul. However, soul has the capability to recognize its true friend and ally. Soul and the mind have lost many battles, but soul and the Master,0 together, always win the war.

SECTION II

FROM LIGHT

TO SOUND

CHAPTER 5

LIGHT AND SOUND IN
THREE GREAT RELIGIONS

The inward journey to truth was well known long before any of our current religions existed. The path to truth was created at the beginning of human experience, simultaneous with the creation of the human body. God designed, created, and endowed the human form with soul and spirit and, therefore, life; and created the five-bodied constitution of humanity and the inner and physical planes of experience as well. Soul's return to its Creator requires only the recognition of these simple facts.

The word *religion*, of Latin derivation, means to unite. The genuine purpose of religion is to reunite soul with the Divine, but the human consciousness has become fertile ground for the mind and the ego to create separateness from the God within. The Light and Sound teachings show us how to transcend separateness and achieve union with the higher self, or soul, and the God within. In the original sense of the word, the teachings of Light and Sound conform to the definition of religion; still, when we examine the path, we see little similarity to the many religions of the world. No churches, mosques, priests, temples, or holy texts exist in the Light and Sound—the teachings are brought forth solely for the purpose of explaining God's design to us, so that we can come to know our true selves. Religion can never improve on God's design. The path already is within each of us, placed there so that we can experience truth and find soul and God within. Humans were not made in need of religion, because we are already complete.

All humanity really has one and the same religion—to reunite with the Creator. Our temples are our own bodies, and our priest is soul—the slumbering spiritual consciousness that can see, be, and know truth. When soul becomes weary of many lifetimes in many forms and seeks to discover its own true divinity, these qualities become a living reality in place of sacred scriptures. Soul bathes in the Audible Life Stream constantly, so no baptism is necessary. Soul lives eternally, so what human can save it?

Many great saints, sages, and masters have walked the face of the earth. True Masters of the highest order always teach that God is one; that we all share the same Creator; that we have been created as soul in Its likeness and image; and it is to God that we yearn to return. This is the one, true, eternal religion.

The spiritual journey of self-discovery at the heart of all religions—this mystical, individual experience—is the basic teaching of all great saints and saviors. Speaking to the apostles, Jesus said, *Unto you is given to know the mystery of the Kingdom of God: but unto them that are without, all these things are done in parables. (Mark 4:11).* That is, only a few are able to understand the esoteric or true teachings, and the masses must be taught in a different way. Especially in Jesus' day, in a world of strict moral codes and guidelines for all activity, God was an external concept rather than an internal reality. Not many were prepared for the divine sojourn of soul. The true message of Jesus' teachings had to be hidden in fables, parables, and statements of many meanings, which is true in nearly all religions. And, as in all religions, the teachings of the founder became codified, edited, and misinterpreted as time passed, with rituals and idolatry replacing the purity of the original spiritual message.

Today, as time continues and nations and peoples evolve, the religious notion of spirituality through right behavior is often not enough to satisfy the spiritual yearning of the evolving group of souls who now occupy our planet. True spiritual understanding is never received from studying a sacred text. Unless we undertake the divine, inward journey of soul, our spiritual understanding cannot fully mature. Priests and sacred texts can all transmit knowledge about spiritual matters, but understanding and realizing such knowledge is obtained only through the journey of one's experience within.

In considering how three great religions express the spiritual energies of Light and Sound, there are four important elements to keep in mind. The first is the religion's founder, whose life and experience cannot be totally separated from the teaching and, thus, are impressed upon the correlated religion. Second, we must survey the outer form of the religion—the teachings as they are presented to the masses of followers as guidelines for living life in the physical world. Third, we must recognize the esoteric or mystical side of the religion, relating to the divine journey of soul. Finally, every religion has a philosophy which appeals to the intellect. We will consider these four factors as we investigate Light and Sound in the three great religions of Buddhism, Christianity, and Islam.

Buddhism

> *What they [the Western public] recognize as Buddhism is a system of wonderful ethics, couched in the most beautiful and poetic language; they recognize in it these moral teachings coupled with rare liberality of thought, with constant appeal to the reason.*
>
> Annie Besant
> 1847 – 1923
> Theosophist, author of *Seven Great Religions*

Buddhism is the most popular religion in the world today. Its founder, Siddhartha, was born sometime around 563 B.C. in the valley of Ganga in India. He was a prince; and his parents, wanting his kingdom to be of this earth, attempted to shield him from the miseries of the world. Siddhartha married early, fathered a child, and then, slipping out of his parents' tight control, became aware of the suffering that surrounded him. He left his family and his inheritance to go out into the world and attempt to end its suffering.

Siddhartha first studied under several well-known philosophers of his day, but could not find the cure he sought for the suffering he saw. He aligned himself with several ascetics who practiced denial of food, sex, etc., as a means of spiritual advancement, but found himself unable to quench his spiritual thirst in this manner. Next, Siddhartha attempted pure contemplation. He sat down beside the sacred Bodhi tree (the tree of wisdom) until enlightenment descended upon him. It was there under the Bodhi tree, we are told, where Siddhartha became the Enlightened One, the Buddha. He realized many births and deaths were necessary to overcome sorrow, and that enlightenment could become real by the total extinction of desires. He envisioned the noble eightfold path which could lead to freedom, and further stated:

> I have penetrated this doctrine which is profound, difficult to perceive and to understand, which brings quietude of heart, which is exalted, which is unattainable by reasoning, abstruse, and intelligible only to the wise.

Buddhist Suttas

Buddha taught that the way to enlightenment required the absence of the passions of the mind (anger, lust, greed, attachment, and vanity) and the complete absence of desire. He also said that this state of consciousness is unattainable by reason. What Buddha termed the "chain of desire" begins with birth, inevitably leads to desires (physical, astral, causal, mental), and eventually to decay and death. His main point, that desire is the source of all evils, was neither new nor unique in world religion—the Vedas, pre-Hindu writings, had stated as much thousands of years earlier.

After Buddha's experience under the Bodhi tree, he began his spiritual mission. He taught that self-indulgence and self-denial were both extremes, and that the middle path, the path of moderation, was the road to wisdom. This eightfold path is represented by right belief, right aspiration, right speech, right conduct, right livelihood, right endeavor, right memory, and right meditation. He emphasized that clinging to the physical senses and their gratification leads to suffering and continued rebirth in this world, and that as we are made free by the absence of passion, then rebirth in this world (the physical plane) is no longer required.

Buddha was a pure man, exuding wisdom and compassion. He taught those who would hear him and initiated many followers into his order. The disciples were required to surrender all possessions, wear the yellow robes of the order, and beg for alms in the streets of India. Since he was born a Hindu and his followers were Hindu, he spoke to them in ways that related to the sacred Hindu texts. He believed that poverty was the proper life for a priest, that to be passionless was the mark of a true man of God, and that the Brahmin (priestly) class had fallen into disrepute and was rife with corruption and the passions of the mind. Although he was largely able to avoid confronting them, he despised the fact that most Brahmins were much more involved with seeking riches and physical pleasures than spiritual truth. He held up the ancient ideal of the priest, created by the Vedic culture before the Brahmins, and challenged them to uphold its standards. He did not succeed in this lofty aim. After his death, his followers attacked the Brahmins even more directly; and Buddhists were driven from India.

Today, Buddhism is split into factions. The two main factions, the Southern Church and the Northern Church, both seem to represent some of the esoteric message Buddha taught: that soul reincarnates in the world to attain perfection; that soul is an individual spark of God and lives within humans continuously. Also included in Buddha's teachings are the two ancient concepts of discrimination (the mental quality of separating the worldly from the spiritual) and detachment (indifference to the world and to the fruits of our actions).

Many modern-day Buddhists believe that Nirvana (heaven) is a great void where life is homogenous and individuality is not present. Reading Buddha's teachings closely (assuming they were correctly recorded and translated) reveals quite the opposite. Buddha yearned for his students to unfold spiritually to the point where further reincarnation on earth was not necessary. Nirvana, as he experienced it, was a state of permanence beyond the changing world in which we live—much more a reality than the non-reality of the void.

Our purpose here is neither to discredit nor debase Buddhism or any other religious or metaphysical path. All have their purposes in the grand scheme of life, and all have their value. Like all religions, as Buddhism spread throughout the world over time, it became diluted; and much of its intended message and spirituality has been lost or codified into dogma.

In surveying Buddhism, we must remember that all religions and metaphysical systems of belief suffer from misinterpretation following the death of their founders. Many of Buddha's teachings, if properly understood, are very much in line with Light and Sound principles. For instance, he openly taught the law of karma and the reincarnation of soul into many bodies over long periods of time. He also realized that the spiritual state of consciousness could neither be won nor perpetuated by asceticism or self-denial. He further realized, through his own experimentation, that philosophy alone would never bring him the enlightenment he desired. His central teaching—that human desires inevitably lead to human suffering, a greater karmic debt, and rebirth in the world—is congruent with the principles of Light and Sound.

In its ethical teaching, Buddhism teaches that desires are never satiated and that only wisdom brings contentment. This is a lofty and noble truth. However, Buddha's method of attaining high ethics and virtues is where he parts company with the Masters of Light and Sound. His teachings stress: "Avoid doing wicked actions; practice most perfect virtue; thoroughly subdue your mind."

Although the Masters of Light and Sound also teach ethics of the highest sort—charity, kindness, right speech and conduct, honesty, truthfulness, and love for all life—they do not teach that we need to thoroughly subdue either the mind or its desires. These Masters realize that unchecked desire leads to suffering, and that, therefore, our worldly desires should be brought into balance, not eradicated. Attempting to free oneself from all human desires and vices is really a level of moralism or a learned, mental viewpoint rather than spirituality. For example, saying that cigarettes are bad and that non-smoking is good is strictly a moral judgment. Health concerns aside, such desires are neither inherently good nor bad; it is the mind which creates such distinctions. The attempt to purify the mind by extinguishing all its desires is still a limited goal that leads us to expend all our vital energies by fighting the battle of good and bad at the level of the mind, while the mind's source of morals depends on its conditioning and the society in which it functions.

It is enough to bring our desires into balance to a point where they no longer compulsively control our behavior. For example, three packs of cigarettes a day may be too much. But rather than trying to quit altogether, two or three cigarettes a day would bring one's desire to smoke into balance. The Masters prefer this approach to our desires because it frees up our attention for spiritual pursuits, rather than limiting it to the mental question of good and evil.

Buddha taught that spiritual liberation could be won by right action and right behavior. Although this course of action may bring a higher vibration within the human consciousness, it will not bring us to true spiritual consciousness. The Masters of Light and Sound seek the purification of the mind, but in a slightly different way than Buddhism: the cure for human desires lies within the Audible Life Stream, the Sound Current, wherein lies the essence of God and all truth, wisdom, and love. Uniting with this essence leaves less energy to fuel the desires which so often distract the truth seeker. The Masters of Light and Sound connect us with this Sound Current. So leading a wholesome life is one thing, and coming in contact with the Divine Spirit within is quite another. This contact with the essence of God purifies the mind and eventually brings desires into balance. The Audible Life Stream ushers us into the fullness of spiritual consciousness and the balancing, not the destruction, of lower desires.

Buddhism's social orientation and goals for world peace and universal brotherhood are noble indeed. The Masters certainly teach universal love, charity, and kindness to others; yet they also teach that unless we are important enough to ourselves, as soul, to seek and gain self-realization and God realization first and foremost, then we will never be able to truly help others to the maximum of their potential. The Masters of Light and Sound, unconcerned with social institutions, seek the spiritual liberation of soul by providing soul the opportunity and method of genuine spiritual liberation, which far exceeds the happiness of the human state of consciousness.

If one truly wants to be happy and avoid suffering, Buddha taught, one only need go within—take the divine journey of soul. This happiness will not be merely the opposite of suffering; it will be the divine bliss which is encountered when the duality of the human consciousness is transcended and the spiritual consciousness is born.

Christianity

> *He that heareth my Word...*
> > *hath everlasting life, and...*
> > *is passed from death unto life. (John 5:24)*

> *If ye had known me*
> > *ye should have known my Father also;*
> > *and from henceforth you know him,*
> > *and have seen him...*
> *He that hath seen me hath seen the Father. (John 14:7,9)*

> *I am the light of the world;*
> > *he that followeth me shall not walk in darkness*
> > *but shall have the light of life. (John 8:12)*

Jesus
Master of Light and Sound

Christianity has become one of the more external and outwardly directed religions in the world today. Conflicting belief systems in Christian denominations have often usurped the great Master Jesus' message. Many wars have been fought and much blood has been shed over its intellectual interpretation, creating a bitterness among many Christians that exists to this day. Christianity is almost unique among religions in its claim to be the one true faith and revelation of God. This claim, of course, creates resentments about who is the true defender of the faith among denominations, as well as with other religions, and even among the non-religious. It is extremely doubtful that Jesus intended anything of the sort.

So much has been said and written about the life of Jesus that little need be said regarding his physical life. His mission began about the age of thirty. He was the living Master of his time for only three years. Much has been made of his use of miracles (healing, restoring sight, etc.), but all Masters have the capability to master physical nature, should they choose to use it. Jesus himself gave little value to this phenomenon. While speaking to his disciples, he said, *Greater works than these shall ye do.*

Jesus' moral and ethical precepts and teachings, though aimed at a specific audience, are perfectly in line with what all great

Masters always have and still do teach:

Love your enemies, bless them that curse you, do good to them that hate you, and pray for them that despitefully use you and persecute you; that ye may be the children of your Father which is in heaven: for he maketh his sun to rise on the evil and the good, and sendeth rain on the just and the unjust. (Matthew 5:44,45).

Charity, truthfulness, and unconditional love, coupled with humility and forgiveness, were beautifully stated in Jesus' parables. Jesus taught well and firmly understood that only by purity in thought, word, and deed can the Pure be seen. *Blessed are the pure in heart: for they shall see God. (Matthew 5:8).*

There can be no doubt that Jesus understood love to be the true essence of soul and the center of genuine religion. When Peter, the disciple, came to Jesus and asked if forgiving another man seven times was enough for certain actions against him, *Jesus saith unto him, 'I say not unto thee until seven times, but until seventy times seven' (Matthew 18:21,22).* By his own example, Jesus taught love for all humans, and, above all, for the God within. He was an avowed anti-materialist who pointed out the need for but little food, some shelter, a few articles of clothing, and a heart that knew no bounds: *This is my commandment, that ye love one another. (John 15:12).*

All Jesus' teachings are based on the principle of sacrifice. Realizing the dual nature of humans, he also recognized the soul and spiritual consciousness within and how the human consciousness shields, perverts, and dims the light of soul. His parables and teachings call on followers to sacrifice the lower self so that the Christ, the soul within each of us, can come to the fore. As all true Masters teach, the type of sacrifice taught by Jesus involves changing our point of view from the object of lower desires to the third eye: *The light of the body is the eye: if therefore thine eye be single, thy whole body shall be full of light. (Matthew 6:22).*

Centering our attention at the third eye leads to the birth of the spiritual consciousness. Jesus knew this well and stated this principle throughout his teachings: *Straight is the gate, and narrow is the way, which leadeth unto life, and few there be that find it. (Matthew 7:14).* The gate that leads within to spiritual truth is the third-eye center. The narrow way is the ancient path which leads to wisdom and love. Jesus continually spoke of his kingdom as being an inner experience, and of spiritual reality being discovered through the journey of soul. He pointed out, though, that "few there be that find it." He realized that the narrow way is one of sacrifice, and that not many are genuinely interested in the birth of spiritual consciousness, due to the need to transcend human consciousness to reach the spiritual self. The great love of God, all life, and spiritual truth, which are the cornerstones of his message, are all attained by the inner journey of soul.

The Christianity we know today is a moralistic teaching. Keeping the ten commandments, being kind and charitable, and leading a sound moral life says much more about "Christianity" and its followers than about the teachings of Jesus himself. The Christian religion was not given to the world by Jesus, but by Paul. Paul transformed Jesus' original message of spiritual self-sacrifice into the Christianity that depicts Jesus as the savior who sacrificed himself on the cross to wash away the sins of humankind. As Julian Johnson states in *The Path of the Masters*, "The real mission of Jesus, which was to lead his disciples to realize the kingdom of heaven within themselves, was turned into a bloody tragedy." Sadly, Jesus' message was not really understood by his own disciples, let alone the spiritually uneducated masses. He was despised for the very purity he lived and taught, and was slain by those who saw his example reflect their own smallness and lack of purity.

Mainstream Christianity has become a teaching centered on the person of Jesus and his divine sacrifice to redeem the world—that he was the *only* son of God, and that *only* by believing this doctrine and adhering to the moral precepts of the church can eternal life be won. This put Jesus on a pedestal that no one could ever touch or even know. With this type of religious philosophy as a backdrop, we can easily see how self-righteous moralism became Church doctrine and led to the Pope becoming emperor of all Europe in six short centuries. As time proceeded, the doctrines of Jesus were increasingly misconstrued, misinterpreted, and purposely misused to empower the Church and control the masses. Dogma replaced doctrine; and truth became buried under an avalanche of ritualism, formalism, and codified law.

In surveying Christianity, we must recognize that the doctrine and dogma of Christianity and the teachings of Jesus, the Master, are mutually exclusive. For example, many accept the belief that Jesus had extensive contact and training with the mystical orders of his day, where he was taught by both the Magi of Mesopotamia and the Essenes—esoteric orders based on ancient principles of Light and Sound—and his spiritual experiences with them formed the core of his teachings. In contrast, the moralism, commandments, and church dogma in Christianity today were largely written by Paul to make the new religion more acceptable to Jews and non-Jews alike.

Despite Christianity's viewpoint of heaven being a reward in the afterlife for a well-lived life on earth, the original teachings of Jesus state quite the contrary. He not only taught that heaven exists here and now, he also taught how to attain self-realization and God realization within this lifetime. The Good Shepherd and Prince of Peace taught that heaven is a kingdom within, that its stages are clearly marked, and that the journey—to which *all* men and women are invited—begins with faith. Faith in God and the kingdom within, coupled with a true Master and genuine, active seeking on the part of the disciple, lead to knowledge. This knowledge is not obtained through reading or study, but through direct spiritual experience of the Audible Life Stream and the spiritual consciousness within us all.

Jesus fully realized that heaven is here and now, and he expected several of his closest disciples to make the effort to achieve the awakening of the spiritual consciousness in their lifetimes. *There be some standing here, which shall not taste of death, till they see the kingdom of God. (Luke 9:27).* All true Masters always have and always will hold this golden promise before their followers. Jesus realized that although many are called and few are chosen, all humankind has the divine potential to withdraw their energies inward from the injustice and passion of the world to the third-eye center and awaken to the Sound Current. *Now ye are clean through the Word of which I have spoken to you. (John 15:3).*

Jesus called the divine Sound *the Word*, the ultimate purifier of the consciousness. All Masters of Light and Sound have endlessly stated and restated this simple truth. The Sound Current, the Word, is the essence of God; and we come to realize spiritual truth and attain salvation by bathing in this divine stream. The divine Sound brings a purity of mind and heart that neither moral codes nor ritual could ever produce. While confession may benefit the heart and mind, soul demands the Word. True baptism in the Holy Spirit can never be conferred by priests or ministers—only by raising our energies to the third eye and reaching the Audible Life Stream within. Christian theology tells us that the life, suffering, and death of Jesus the Christ provided the final reconciliation between God and man called the atonement. True "at-one-ment" occurs when we reconcile our inner separation from the divine Word, or spiritual energy of Sound, and become "at one" with It.

In Jesus' time, the Roman Empire ruled with an iron hand over the lives of the people of Israel, who desperately longed for a messiah to lead them in battle to remove the Romans from the land of Abraham, Isaac, Elijah, and Moses. But because the transcendental teachings of the great Master were not the answer to their worldly dilemma, most turned their backs on the only genuine hope they had of true salvation and labeled Jesus a dreamer, an idealist, and worse yet, a blasphemer and a heretic. While Jesus taught the principles of Light and Sound, the living Master, and the Audible Life Stream, virtually all of his teachings fell on deaf ears.

Jesus' message included the doctrine of karma and reincarnation. "As ye sow so shall ye reap" is a beautifully simple, yet direct statement of the law of karma that does not refer to reward or punishment in the afterlife. It means that individual souls, when living within the first four planes of existence (physical, astral, mental, causal), are self-regulating entities; and as soul, we are completely responsible for all our actions in life as well as attaining our own salvation. We must sow the seeds or create the conditions which will produce a spiritually abundant harvest. Our reward is not everlasting life in some far-off kingdom of bliss and well-being, but rather union with the God-essence within our own being. Our punishment is not eternal damnation in some fiery pit, but rather experiencing the effects of our own ill-conceived actions until we learn to live in harmony with universal principles.

All karma is remedial, meant to teach and uplift soul. The God that Jesus served so well is a God of infinite compassion, expressing Its willingness to allow soul many lives and many experiences to come into an understanding of itself and the divine principles. This allows us to learn to consciously create what we want and need to live in soul awareness while in a physical body. Reincarnation goes hand in hand with and is inseparable from the law of karma. Direct references to reincarnation were likely deleted from the Bible we know by the infamous Council of Nicea in the fourth century A.D. Many believe that when this council had completed its work, much of Jesus' original message was lost, dogmatized, or misconstrued; and the spiritual beauty of reincarnation of soul and the divine opportunity of the law of karma were manipulated into a doctrine based on fear and punishment.

Without the presence of a living Master, the tenets of any religious or spiritual movement begin to degenerate. We can no more get guidance, direction, and correct understanding and interpretation of truth from a departed Master than a child can get nourishment from a mother who lies in her grave. The Masters of Light and Sound emphatically state that we must have a true, living Master to initiate us into the divine Sound. The great Masters of the past have completed their spiritual missions on earth and moved on to other dimensions and duties. While their work on earth was divinely inspired, gracefully executed, and uplifting to all life, it is always the living Masters of the day who bear the torch of truth. We as seekers must draw closer to that heavenly flame, until we merge with its illuminating light.

Islam

> *Say God is one God.*
> *He begetteth not, neither is He begotten;*
> *and there is not anyone like unto Him.*
>
> The Koran, chapter 112

> *Your deeds alone will be taken into account;*
> *Caste and creed will stand apart uncared for.*
>
> Bulleh Shah
> 18th century Muslim saint
> Disciple of Shah Inayat

Muhammad, the founder of Islam, was born in Mecca in about 571 A.D. At the time of his birth, Arabia was in disarray, plagued by religious wars and fighting between rival factions and clans. Humans were commonly sacrificed to idols. Worshippers ate the bodies of the sacrificed, and lust was on the rise. Muhammad's own father was sacrificed by his grandfather shortly before Muhammad's birth. At twenty-four, Muhammad married Khadija, who later became his first disciple. Following the marriage came many years of inner struggle and strife for Muhammad. He left his home and wife and wandered the vast desert for fifteen years where, we are told, he was visited by an angel who told him, *Rise, thou art the Prophet of God; go forth and cry in the name of the Lord.*

Muhammad was loved and respected in his homeland as a wise, gentle, trustworthy man; he was also illiterate, untrained, and filled with self-doubt about his mission. He felt unworthy of his calling and uncertain as to how to go about it. After he returned home, Khadija helped convince him to follow his calling. Several of the Prophet's close relatives became his next disciples; after three years, his disciples numbered thirty. They spoke glowingly of how he brought greater truth into their lives, forbade the worship of idols, and taught his followers to be merciful, to respect women, to pray, and to fast.

When Muhammad first criticized the people for their drinking, lust, and human sacrifices, many of his disciples were tortured and killed by the angry crowd. Those who survived, however, came to love the Prophet even more. The persecution continued; and shortly after Khadija's death, he and his followers fled to the town of Medina. There his followers increased and after years of continuous struggle, not only with his enemies in Mecca, but among his followers as well, he became ruler of the state.

Muhammad died on June 8, 632 A.D. His favorite disciple, Abu Bekr, then became the head of Islam. Muslim warriors felt it a spiritual honor and a divine road to heaven to die in battle for Islam. Within twenty-five years, the teachings of the Prophet spread by word, war, and political alliances over all of Persia. Over a period of time, Syria, Asia Minor, and many Mediterranean areas also became Islamic.

Every religion comes into the world for a particular purpose. Islam was born at a time of chaos and degeneracy, an era of superstition, lust, and greed, when many gods were worshipped, and might made right. The strict religious codes and disciplines of Islam brought order and stability, while belief in a single god brought a direct, relatively simple, clear-cut theology to a people who needed it.

The word *Islam* means surrendering to the will of God, and perfect submission to divine will is the epitome of Islamic teaching. According to Islam, the extensions of Allah on earth are the prophets, including Abraham, Ishmael, Isaac, Jacob, and Jesus, whom he sends to spread his message. Muhammad, however, is revered as the last true prophet and the greatest of all. The Koran, the book of Islamic spiritual tenets, does not judge other religions. *"Unto God we all return"* is its basic stance, and all blessings lie in the hands of Allah. Since these prophets represented Allah, they too are to be revered and followed. The principle of Islam—surrender—is seen as the one primary tenet, and all who uphold this principle are "children of Islam."

Following Allah in the Islamic hierarchy are the four great archangels, then the recording angels (two to each individual), and finally the minor angels, which surround us to administer divine law and divine will. Both a seven-fold heaven and a seven-fold hell are part of the outer teaching. Like Satan, Iblis is a fallen archangel who rebelled and became man's tempter and the sower of evil seeds.

In Islam, one's foremost duty is righteousness—showing kindness and charity to others out of one's belief in God, the angels, the Koran, and the Prophets; prayer five times a day is also essential. The Koran teaches: *A man's true wealth hereafter is the good he does in this world to his fellow man.* Tenderness towards parents and elders and respect for women and their inherent equality are all part of the Koran. Certain disciplines for the faithful include fasting during the entire month of Ramadan, a pilgrimage to Mecca at least once, giving alms, and daily prayers. Alcohol and drugs are forbidden.

Muhammad taught that knowledge was all important; the Koran states: *The ink of the scholar is more valuable than the blood of the martyr.* This important statement of the Prophet may seem unexpected. Many have fought and died for Islam—as have followers for most major religions. He believed the study of science, the arts, and mmathematics was paramount because it glorified God and led the individual to finer discrimination in determining one's spiritual duty. From the eighth century until the fourteenth century, Islamic culture led the world in its achievements in astronomy, chemistry, mathematics, and architecture. Also, great Arabic philosophers, mystics, and saints from the past abound, including Kabir, Shamas-i-Tabriz, Rumi, Hafiz, and Bulleh Shah. Many of them have not been recognized because of their esoteric, unorthodox approaches to truth.

The mystical, esoteric side of Islam began in the year following the Prophet's flight from Mecca, when what is known today as Sufism began. Sufis practice rigid austerities, but their love of the Divine still shines forth brightly in their inspired verses. A disciple of Sufism is required to have a living teacher; prolonged meditation is used to attain enlightenment; and the path to God is seen as an inward journey. Sufism teaches the existence of one God, that all the universe is but a mirror of It, and that individuals are responsible for their own salvation and their own growth from the human consciousness to the spiritual consciousness from whence they came.

In surveying the religion of Islam, several facts common to all religions stand out. First, there is the holy book, the Koran, believed to contain direct revelation from Allah to Muhammad. Beautifully written and inspired, its contents describe a prescription for correct behavior. This code was well suited to its time and brought a much needed stability to the people who came under its influence.

Islam leans heavily upon the revelations of Muhammad and the authenticity of the Koran for its authority. The truth of the Koran is not being discussed here, only the reliance upon external sources to have truth revealed. Light and Sound, as a teaching, involves an opposite approach: each of us is the path, and truth is discovered through our own efforts and experimentation. The true Master is an inner reality, and the object of the student's efforts is to unite with the God within.

The seven levels of heaven and hell found in Islam are promises of reward and punishment for a good or bad life on earth, while the Light and Sound does not convey moral guidelines for living on earth—the ethics of life are left up to the individual to choose. The major difference, according to most interpretations of Islam, is not in behavior, but in the belief that heaven is a state to be experienced after death and cannot be entered into while still in the physical body. The basic premise of Light and Sound is that spiritual consciousness can only be won when the human state of consciousness is transcended while living in the body. In Light and Sound, heaven, as a spiritual state of consciousness, can and must be attained here and now. Death is not the ticket to heaven, but the ticket to further rebirth in the physical worlds.

The religion of Islam agrees completely with the Masters of Light and Sound that God is one; that God created the many planes and worlds of experience, and utilizes secondary energies (similar to Islam's archangels, though not directly personified) who help in carrying out Its divine plan of creation. Both Islam and the Light and Sound agree that a negative power exists. In Islam, this power (personified as Iblis) is quite similar to what the Christian religion calls Satan—a fallen angel who opposes God and attempts to sway us to greed, lust, anger, vanity, and generally immoral activity. Iblis deals with the polarity of good and bad within the realm of behavior.

The Light and Sound teachings outline the role of the negative power differently: the negative power is not a fallen angel, but is a purposeful tangent of the divine energy present within every mind. Its purpose is to deceive humankind through good and bad alike; and to present humanity with the illusion that the human state of consciousness knows truth and reality, and that the mind and ego are supreme. It uses all the perversions of the mind (lust, anger, vanity, greed, and attachment) as well as the mind's noble virtues to keep individuals connected to the human state of consciousness. It cares little if we are deceived by goodness, kind acts, moral behavior, vices, or anger. As long as we remain within the human state of consciousness and fail to ascend to the spiritual consciousness within, this negative influence within our shared universal mind has been successful.

The basic tenet of Islam is surrender to the will of God; the same is true within the Light and Sound. In traditional Islam, Allah is in a separate heaven, while humans live on earth. The will of Allah is interpreted as right action and correct moral behavior. In contrast, to the follower of a Master of Light and Sound, surrender has little to do with codes of behavior and morals, and much to do with revitalizing the seeing and hearing faculties of soul so the sincere seeker can know, see, and be truth, here and now. Surrender is an internal affair that allows one to let go of the mind, ego, and personality so that soul can reclaim its rulership. Pure religion involves uniting human consciousness with the latent spiritual consciousness within. All external supports exist only until they can be removed; then we can stand on our own feet, guided and directed by the God within us all—the God born of our holy understanding.

CHAPTER 6

PSYCHIC CONSCIOUSNESS

In the initial stages of pursuing the Light and Sound Teachings, pure purpose is impossible, for we simply do not know our deep-lying motives that spur us into action. Everyone has his or her own reason for desiring truth, but usually the motive is tainted with both relief from the misery of the world and seeking some balm to soothe the deep wounds of pain and suffering. Deep in the heart of all truth lovers is the unsettled knowingness that something is missing, and that one's own life and survival depends on finding this something. Humankind searches the world over to find this promised Elixir...this fountain of youth, but the search is futile. In desperation new avenues are trod, new paths are investigated, new loves are embraced, yet the enslavement remains the same.

Sri Gary Olsen
1948 –
Author and Master of Light and Sound

Until one experiences self-realization and God realization, all our living is done within the enormous, indescribable parameters of psychic consciousness. To many, the word *psychic* has a narrow, well-defined meaning—an intuitive sixth sense that allows us to delve into the future or the past of ourselves or others. In reality, the term *psychic* is much broader, more vast, and all-encompassing in its meaning, referring to nearly all the elements of awareness within humankind which we use to survive and live life daily. This "psychic consciousness" does all our thinking and reasoning, and experiences all our emotions; it incorporates all the activity of the physical, astral, causal, and mental bodies. The vast fields of experience and living which have been defined as psychic are indeed staggering. Psychic consciousness deals with all time and space, all incarnations, and all identifications that we use to form the cocoon which covers the beautiful butterfly of soul. Thus, any aspect of consciousness or action that does not originate from the soul body can be termed psychic.

After the Audible Life Stream emerges from the bosom of God to sustain all creation, it reaches the lower worlds of form and matter. Here this great river of the Sound Current divides into the two currents of positive and negative. This creates duality, and all things appear to exist in relation to their opposites. Again, does male have meaning apart from female? Or life, apart from death? Both polarities are necessary for life, existence, and meaning in these lower worlds.

We rely on the duality of positive and negative forces to sustain us in our lives, to create our dreams, and to enslave us in webs of karma and illusion. Living within these boundaries brings relative levels of truth, coupled with an internal dissatisfaction and divine discontent. Relative truth brings emotional joy tempered by moments, days, or years of loneliness and melancholy; it brings the promise of youth, but also the stagnation of routine, and eventually, death. This psychic level of consciousness permeates and dominates the minds of all humankind, including the spiritual seeker. Within the psychic consciousness, many rise up in anger to slay a dragon, topple a windmill, and correct all the wrongs of the world, while others internalize their anger and seethe within. Billions turn to some god or another for a ray of hope; a glimpse of truth, protection, an explanation; or an ounce of true love. Throughout history, humankind has turned toward the heavens in hope, wonder, expectation, and desperation, praying, "There must be something more!"

As souls, we experience countless lifetimes within the confines of this psychic consciousness (the physical, astral, causal, and mental bodies). Try as we may to escape the confinement of the psychic domain, we remain ensnared by its web, trying outlet after outlet, release after release, addiction after addiction, and path after path. Usually our happiness is fleeting, and we retain the haunting feeling that our dream remains unfilled. We reach out for another idea, another system, a new study, a new lifestyle, or a change of locale; and again we realize only partial fulfillment, accompanied by that emptiness to which only the truth seeker can relate. The path to self-realization and God realization is not for the fully contented, the well-adjusted, or the spiritually satiated. It is for those who still search for life's elixir, who still have a dram of belief that it must exist, who remain willing to seek, who have been unable to completely give themselves to anything less.

All spiritual seekers dream of escaping from the confines of the mind, emotions, and entrapping karmic patterns of action and inaction. Truth seekers want freedom and desire to experience soul unfettered; yet try as we may, we appear unable to fulfill our dream. Why? Simply because we have been seeking through the light, or the power of mind and emotions, and although light is powerful enough to reveal the dust and dirt within the home of our own consciousness, it is not powerful enough to remove it. The more it reveals, the further it removes us from soul, truth, and the essential core of our being.

Psychic consciousness is the epitome of light; and it is light, as a spiritual energy, that controls the dual worlds. As beautiful as the light can be, it deceives us, as soul, into accepting a lesser state of being, and living a life that is apart from soul, our true nature, and from the God within.

Light (and therefore, psychic consciousness) derives from Sound and is merely a reflection of Sound. Sound is the true power and remains unseen, unheard, and basically unexperienced within the lower worlds. Because the Sound—the all-sustaining *spiritual* current of consciousness—is latent within us, we turn to the light to provide us with our sustenance, our support, our desires, and our experiences of living. All the lower worlds and lower bodies (physical, astral, causal, mental) are merely reflections of the soul body and its native land, the soul plane. Thus, the light and psychic consciousness only reflect the spiritual beauty and potency of Sound.

Just as a mirror reverses the image it reflects, so does the light energy reverse the image of Sound. In using light, we rely on the feeble agency of our own mind instead of relying on the aid of a true Master to awaken the latent Sound. We know we must go within to discover truth, but psychic consciousness convinces us this inner search is done with mind. Thus, the authentic inner path to soul through the third eye, with the guidance and protection of a true Master, is a journey through the labyrinth of mind and the positive and negative polarities.

The Lure of Psychic Consciousness

Psychic consciousness appeals so strongly to the mind and emotions that we could easily devote several chapters to it, but the basic issue is one of false empowerment. Some people suffer from low self-esteem, and a little bit of knowledge and perhaps the development of a few psychic powers goes a long way in propping up a deflated ego. Through this insidious means, psychic consciousness, or attachment to knowledge and information, grips the seeker, ensnaring us in its illusory web. The psychic knowledge and powers may be real enough in themselves; it is the seeker's interpretation of the value of such knowledge that leads to a sense of false empowerment.

The lure of the psychic consciousness works through our mind's attempts to experience spiritual awareness and to mentally "understand" spiritual truth. Because soul's divine ability to know, be, and see truth is shrouded and underdeveloped, we substitute the mind's desire for knowledge and the emotions' desire for feeling for soul's innate love, power, and wisdom. The mind is curious and often impatient. We frantically set out to explain our outer and inner worlds through study and countless questions, feeling that the answers to our questions will bring spiritual truth. We often feel we are on the brink of understanding; and if we could only get the answer to just one more question, the puzzle would be solved.

The appeal of the psychic consciousness overwhelms the minds of even the most sincere seekers. Psychic paths, religions, and metaphysical studies all claim to have answers. The allure of these claims can be compared with letting a child loose in a toy store with a no-limit credit card. Hope of answers for our questions and the promise of the secrets of the universe are very tempting bait indeed. The most alluring aspect of the psychic paths lies in the fact that they actually can deliver answers to some questions. A genuine psychic reader can tell you things about your past that you've already forgotten, and predict your future with uncanny accuracy. Many competent people in the psychic arts can tell you more about your health than your doctor. A professional astrologer may reveal more about the workings of your mind than a highly paid psychologist or psychiatrist. Such knowledge can go a long way to satisfy the mind's insistent need to know, as well as provide more fodder for further questioning and speculation. Mind loves nothing more than this.

Often, as our metaphysical knowledge or psychic abilities increase, we mistake this expanded experience for genuine soul awakening. However, all answers from within psychic consciousness are incomplete; none provides the pure truth that brings the spiritual liberation the seeker craves. The mind and the emotions—not soul—stand to gain the most from psychic influence by only dealing with the specific development of the astral, causal, and mental bodies. Questions arising from the mind only produce answers that come from the mind. No amount of knowledge of light can be an adequate substitute for the pure understanding which the awakening of the latent Sound Current delivers.

All seeking which increases "metaphysical" knowledge belongs to the dominion of light; and although such seeking has relative value and benefit, it is only one step on the ladder of soul's unfoldment, and certainly is not the ultimate destination. The overall effect of engaging in work which deals with the psychic consciousness is to waylay soul into unnecessary tangents, which hold out much hope but end up leading us away from that which we are truly seeking.

As the New Age movement continues to gain momentum, it attracts an ever-increasing following; and the allurement of joining, being contemporary, being fashionable, and participating with an "in" crowd will exert both overt and subtle influences on the mind and emotions. Humans are much more of a herd animal than we would care to think. The appeal of fad-following, being hip, and being one who is supposedly in the know cannot be underestimated; it boosts the ego and provides a warm, calming effect to the emotions, allowing for an enriched but temporary feeling of well-being. Being a follower is a greater temptation than being one who seeks an individual truth within. Few are truly comfortable standing apart from the crowd, unable to feed on the energy of pseudo-togetherness that the psychic states of consciousness provide.

Another seductive appeal of psychic consciousness is the apparent fulfillment of the ego's tremendous need for love and acceptance. In our haste to experience love, we quite often settle for lesser forms of love while soul's true spiritual love remains untapped. A teacher, psychic path, pseudo-guru, or love of ceremony and ritual all become such strong magnets for our affection that we expend all our vital energies in a love affair with the light.

The mind loves knowledge; the ego loves approval, acceptance, and self-value; and the emotions love to emote! But is this how we wish to fulfill our needs? If we allow the psychic consciousness to fulfill our emotional needs for love, we will never know the greater love of soul. If we allow our love affair with knowledge, even knowledge of a "spiritual" nature, to sustain us, we risk missing the discovery of pure truth within, via awakening the latent Sound Current. It is the spiritual energy of Sound, the all-embracing river of God, that we unknowingly seek. Yet in our true desire for greater spirituality, we often become captivated by the lure of the energy of light, much like a child who buys a shiny but poorly constructed toy to take home—a toy that captivates, but soon falls apart.

Another powerful appeal of psychic consciousness relates to the predictive arts, such as astrology, tarot, palmistry, and aura reading, that deal with the future and our anxieties about it. Whether or not the information we receive from a given psychic is true, it appeals to the mind and the emotions and promotes the survival of the ego, even bolstering and defending it. With our anxieties lessened, we experience temporary contentment within human consciousness, and keep our concerns and attention riveted there, at great cost to soul.

Human consciousness is riddled with feelings of separateness and alienation, so seekers who align themselves with psychic consciousness often feel it to be some higher power or spiritual force. Because the origin of psychic power is the light itself, seekers experience its warmth through a particular guide, channeler, natural energy, or universal force. Given our loneliness and desire to merge with something greater than our own ego, these psychic forces provide solace for the unwary. Because we do not know that there are forces of a much higher origin than these, such identifications can lessen our sense of alienation and create a sense of harmony with the mysterious forces around us. As appealing as external methods and limited goals may be, the truth seeker awaits and desires the greater goals of self-realization and God realization. Other efforts of uniting and merging with higher forces may provide temporary relief from separateness, but eventually will prove to be illusory and incomplete because they are products of light. Sound and soul remain unawakened.

Many seekers validate the afterlife through psychic means, and find peace and contentment in the knowledge of eternal life. This perfectly understandable point of view of human consciousness is also very limiting. It may superficially serve to eliminate the fear of death, but what help is it in soul's quest for liberation? The mere knowledge of the immortality of soul does little to free it from the bondage and enslavement under which it currently exists. In fact, soul's bondage to the senses actually increases when those who have pierced the veil feel falsely free and unencumbered, merely due to their knowledge that life goes on. Unless spiritual consciousness is won and self-realization is experienced, the soul remains trapped within the confines of psychic consciousness and the lower bodies, even after physical death.

The paths which solely employ the light masquerading as redemption lure many with promises of increased well-being, happiness, spiritual awareness, and sacred knowledge. While these promises may be valid in one sense, they lack in another. Paths that rely on light and the vast levels of psychic consciousness contain elements of truth. This awareness brings tidbits of spiritual understanding and fleeting feelings of harmony and well-being, and yet our entrapment remains the same. Although psychic consciousness seems to lead to the center of our being, in fact, it leads us farther from our center into distorted tangents, lesser reflections, and partial revelations.

Psychic Paths, Practices, and Influences: Steps on the Ladder of Soul's Unfoldment

The spiritual energy of light and psychic consciousness often provides a necessary step in unfoldment, a new burst of faith or hope, new insights, even renewed inspiration to delve deeper into the mysteries of the Divine. However, there comes a time when the light has fulfilled its spiritual purpose. Perhaps the most valuable gift that psychic consciousness can give the truth seeker is the desire to escape its confines!

All psychic approaches to spiritual unfoldment contain an external element. Rather than approaching truth directly through the divine inner journey of soul, they use an outside prop to activate one's search: astrology uses horoscopes, tarot uses cards, and palmistry uses lines on the hand. With any type of spiritualism, a medium is employed as well as the disembodied entity that is being contacted. By relying on outside sources to provide the truth, the follower often becomes dependent on exterior sources.

Several other dangers are present in all psychic practices because of involvement with external elements. Psychic approaches to spirituality provide us with a limited point of view, at best. Truth is a relative concept in the lower worlds, and its relative perspectives all deal with our lower bodies, leaving the soul body unrevealed. This often leads us to believe that the great goals of self-realization and God realization can be won through good acts, moral behavior, information gleaned through psychic and metaphysical studies, or by divine intervention of a god who will deliver spiritual salvation to us, just for the asking.

Psychic approaches deal with secondhand knowledge and information, so the qualifications of the reader, channeler, medium, or astrologer are always in question. Deception and illusion are the order of the day in the physical world as well as in the astral, causal, and mental planes of experience. Without directly challenging the honesty of those involved in the psychic fields, we should be aware of the possibility of misrepresentation, exaggeration, and false information and promises as we continue our search.

The value of any path is determined by its origin. Just as a master who is not sufficiently developed spiritually cannot lead seekers to self-realization and God realization, neither can a psychic path in the lower planes bring seekers to truths that lie beyond its reach. Psychic paths can provide valuable information regarding the workings of the personality, the ego, the mind, the subconscious, and the emotional body; but true spiritual freedom and attainment lie beyond the scope of psychic awareness. Once one has fully experienced the psychic paths, little attraction to such knowledge remains, for the seeker will realize that psychic awareness, or light, is only a reflection of pure truth, and that the spiritual energy of Sound can be experienced directly through the inner journey of soul.

Astrology

We are born at a given moment, in a given place, and like vintage years of wine, we have the qualities of the year and of the season in which we are born. Astrology does not lay claim to anything more.

Carl Jung
1875 – 1961
20th century psychologist, author

The celestial bodies are the cause of all that takes place in the sublunar world.

Thomas Aquinas
1225 – 1274
13th century theologian, philosopher

Astrology, when properly applied, provides great insight into our thought processes and knowledge about the mind and its workings, emotional responses, health, finances, sexuality, and the personality of its users. Some advanced astrology even deals with the overriding karmic burdens of the individual, and attempts to give specific meaning to the particular challenges the individual faces in this lifetime.

Astrology maps out potent, prevailing character traits which bind us to our lower selves, if unchecked. It describes the limited viewpoint of mind and the illusions under which it currently operates in fairly accurate terms. Sadly, many people consider astrology to be a pseudo-science, neither grounded in empirical data nor supported by scientific method. The modern world largely fails to see the importance of astrology (and indeed, many other psychic arts) because they have been so commercialized and simplified for the mass market. Astrology provides a valuable glimpse into the mechanics of the state of human consciousness, and leads sincere seekers to further explore the realms of awareness within themselves.

At a deeper level, though, people often resent being categorized in any way. In the human state of consciousness, we feel we possess free will and are unencumbered in our thinking; that we are independent and uniquely individual. We like to feel that we can think and respond rationally to situations, that the mind is fluid, and that ego presents no real barrier or boundary to our expressions. Astrology explains just how limited our thinking can be and how compartmentalized the mind and personality actually are.

How does astrology help in correcting our deficiencies or overcoming the particular mind set with which we are born? Basically, it suggests that we substitute one mental or emotional quality for another, or temper our negative personality traits with a dose of positive traits. This exercise in substitution yields only partial and temporary results, but cannot truly provide the deep, permanent inner change in consciousness we so ardently desire. Astrology can bring greater knowledge of the workings of the mind, the composition of character and personality, and the emotional responses which influence behavior, while soul, which lives, breathes, and acts in the realm of the spiritual consciousness, is left untouched. The help and guidance of even the world's greatest astrologers cannot adequately substitute for the spiritual food we find at the table of a true Master.

The Pop Guru

If the blind lead the blind, both fall in the ditch. (Matthew 15:14)

Jesus
Master of Light and Sound

Life in the late twentieth century has become increasingly tech-nological and often highly detrimental to our planet and the sur-rounding atmosphere. People such as Lynn Andrews, Sun Bear, and Robert Boissiere point to a need to return to a more balanced and har-monious lifestyle which reflects a respect for all life and the earth itself. Such information and knowledge provide a conduit for greater light and general upliftment of all life. The Divine Itself has seen fit to pre-sent such awareness to our society at this time; its value is obvious.

Pop gurus have developed sufficient light within themselves to be able to capture the attention, imagination, and allegiance of the masses. (In fairness to those individuals, the term "pop guru" is a creation of the media and not a self-selected title.) One trip to your local metaphysical bookstore reveals the fact that our society now accepts and supports literally thousands of individuals as "givers of light." Generally, the Masters of Light and Sound applaud and wel-come the heightened interest in psychic matters that is emerging in the world today. A true Master well understands the suffering and alienation that we all experience in the human state of consciousness, and realizes that seekers generally exhaust most avenues of psychic development before arriving at his doorstep. The explosion of psy-chic paths and spiritual teachers only hastens the journey of many truth seekers, allowing seekers to be drawn more quickly to a path where their particular spiritual needs can be met, transcended, or replaced by more transformative spiritual truths.

All religions, psychic paths, and pop gurus have their places and particular meanings in the Creator's scheme of life and spiritual unfoldment. The Masters of Light and Sound are very aware of this simple fact and continually point to the inherent value of such steps on the ladder of soul's awakening, as well as the limitations and par-tial perspective or viewpoint from each rung on the ladder. The old axiom that half-knowledge is dangerous is true in spiritual life as well as the physical. Although psychic paths and pop gurus can pro-vide a valuable learning experience, they also can mislead and ensnare unwary seekers in a net of illusion.

For example, many of them have taught others to use the word *OM* as a "power" word that best duplicates the vibration of God. However, OM is a vibrational frequency encountered in the mental plane, associated with Brahm, the Hindu name for the "overlord" of the universal mind power from which all individual minds are derived. If seekers utilize the power and vibration of the OM chant, they can then easily believe that the true God power within has been contacted, when in fact they have only experienced increased universal mind power (the light). Such a serious mistake often has dire consequences. While it certainly may increase vibrations within the human state of consciousness and provide upliftment, it only puts one in touch with the higher aspects of the mind, or the light, while soul, true center of one's being, is yet to be contacted or experienced.

The purpose of the negative power is to deceive. The first four planes, the psychic regions, are filled with illusions—half-truths abound; things are not what they appear to be; and purposeful deceit is prevalent, even rampant. The psychic regions are the most treacherous in all the universal body of the Divine. Many spiritual teachers of the day are captivated by the allurement of the light and are sharing their partial truths with an unwary, spiritually unsophisticated public, which is responding in droves.

Attempting to journey unescorted through these planes of consciousness is ill-conceived at best, and often leads seekers further astray. The psychic teachings and the pop gurus, appealing as they may be, cannot measure up to the guidance of a true Master. Without the Master's aid to expose the illusory nature of the lower psychic planes, sincere seekers are simply unprepared to successfully wage war with the armada of illusions that the psychic worlds contain. A true Master stands atop the ladder of soul's continuing unfoldment and, from this lofty perch of enlightenment, can easily see the relative truth of any given experience of spiritual endeavor as well as its inherent limitations or dangers. The Masters seek not to create better conditions within our self-created prison, but to free us altogether.

The Goddess Energy

Tremendous interest has developed recently in goddess energy—the feelings, thoughts, and power of the feminine principle. The rise in interest and expression of the goddess energy is not surprising; fueling widespread social and political changes, it is rooted in both recent history and spiritual law.

Historically, human culture has generally been male-dominated; and the control of wealth, capital, and business and political power has been largely a male experience. Until very recently, women's only place has been in the home; and her role in the household and in society at large has been one of subservience, playing second fiddle, and always acting in support of the patriarchal head. Only in this century were women in the U.S. granted the most basic political right—the right to vote. The past twenty-five years has bred widespread changes in the outer structure of our society, as well as within the fabric itself. The rise of feminism—supporting working women, single mothers, gay rights, civil rights, and the rights of all living species and their ecosystems—can be correlated with an upsurge in recognizing and implementing the feminine principle.

The increased interest in the feminine principle has allowed both genders to re-evaluate their blend and balance of the masculine and feminine currents, or lack of it; this is a first step. Today, however, well-meaning spiritual seekers are deluding themselves by elevating the feminine principle to the same heights to which the masculine principle had been falsely elevated, and many people are turning toward the feminine principle as their deliverer. Although this backlash of concern is understandable in a society where the strengths of the feminine principle have been largely ignored, we cannot afford such over-compensation based on the same duality.

The tremendous allure and drawing power of the feminine principle lies in its association with giving birth, creating, and nurturing. Virtually all religions and cultures have paid homage to the feminine principle through various goddesses. The Great Mother has been worshipped in Egypt, Europe, Scandinavia, Polynesia, and North and South America. In India there are Kali and Shakti, the great mother goddess. The Greeks and Romans personalized the goddess energy in Ceres, Athena, Venus, and Aphrodite. In Africa there is the Rain Goddess; and in China, the Mother Goddess. Catholicism adopted the ancient Hindu and Egyptian model of the savior born of a virgin and created the Virgin Mary as the mother goddess, the ultimate protector, nourisher, and miracle worker.

While the feminine principle may be responsible for creation and destruction in the lower worlds, it is not the prime origin of creation. The Sound creates both the feminine and masculine principles, both energies of light! The Audible Life Stream or Sound Current, which issues forth from the Heart of God, ultimately creates and sustains life on all planes of existence. To revere, worship, or idolize Mother Nature, the Virgin Mary, or any other form of goddess energy is again more illusion, equal to worshipping only a male figure. Although the masculine and feminine currents are valuable energies for the seeker to understand and utilize, both are actually only minor streams of energy in the universal body of God. They deserve our attention to gain the knowledge their existence can impart. They do not deserve our worship.

Channeled Entities

To the general public, trance channeling—a medium who enters briefly into a self-induced trance state and allows a visiting entity to speak, heal, or act through the medium—is probably among the most captivating aspects of the so-called New Age. Several channels currently working in this field claim to be channels for great departed artists; others state that they are empowered by higher entities to heal or perform psychic surgery. Trance channels are mediums for information and knowledge; and while such information may be highly elevated, it is still within the confines of the light.

Trance channeling certainly is not new, having been practiced in nearly every known society and culture. The shamanic tradition is rich with examples of healers and seers who channel energies or messages from guiding spirits. Societies around the globe have recognized and utilized the psychic abilities of men and women to act as receivers and transmitters of prophecy, healing energy, knowledge, and information.

A seeker can be virtually assaulted by the explosion of information from channeled entities such as Ramtha, Lazarus, the Space Brothers, the Guides, and thousands of others. Whom do we believe? Whose message is accurate, and whose is self-deluded or fraudulent? These questions face many sincere spiritual seekers as they attempt to sift spiritual truth from silos of metaphysical speculation. Rather than being concerned about the validity of the information or the channeler, let us inspect the principle which supports the need for such information and the methods of obtaining it.

The mind desires to seek truth through knowledge; this motivates many to seek the information provided through the psychic senses. Those who seek truth through greater knowledge and information have identified themselves as the mind and not as soul. They see themselves as limited, basically ignorant of truth, and as having large gaps in knowledge. In contrast, soul needs no greater knowledge, for it contains all truth. Soul's only need is union with God, for it is already imbued with the divine attributes of love, wisdom, freedom, and spiritual power. While the mind searches for greater light, soul is sourced by the awakening of Sound.

Reliance on external psychic paths always involves secondhand knowledge; in trance channeling, there is even a third party. Is the channeled entity reliable? Is the channeler receiving and transmitting accurately? The seeker has virtually no way of answering these questions. Fraud is often encountered within the psychic fields, yet some degree of self-delusion is even more common among the practitioners of psychic phenomena. Strong desire and belief in the principle of genuine psychic contact allow many psychics and trance channels to receive and transmit information and impressions from their own minds, mistaking the products of their own imagination for authentic psychic reality. Much of the so-called channeled information offered to the public today is primarily self-delusion.

Certain channels actually do channel information from entities residing on the psychic planes (astral, causal, mental), providing a sometimes necessary step on the ladder of soul unfoldment by validating the existence of the afterlife, and introducing the law of karma and the principle of reincarnation. This knowledge can awaken the desire to further explore the mysteries of life, or kindle a desire to explore metaphysics.

Eventually, as the seeker begins to tire of mental revelation, a yearning for direct experience begins to replace the stimulation to the mind and emotions provided by psychism. Although the seeker can enjoy and even profit by these interactions with the light, they do not provide true, divine knowledge—that of soul, the real self. Pure truth can never be found by externally searching within the lower worlds. Neither the beautiful mind nor sweet emotions can deliver us to truth's door. Only soul is fine enough to penetrate the keyhole to the door of truth; only soul resonates with the same exquisite vibration found within the Creator's courtyard.

There comes a time in each of our lives when we put away the toys of our childhood. The same is true in our spiritual journey and endeavor. Eventually, all lower, dualistic, limited approaches to truth lose their power and appeal in captivating our attention. We eventually grow weary of reality as the dual worlds present it, as the light alone no longer nourishes our desires to unfold and progress spiritually. All psychic, religious, and metaphysical approaches to truth reveal a portion of its glory, while the higher and purer spirit of divine truth eludes the grasp of our senses. Truth is hidden in the last place we would ever search—within our own precious body, the temple of soul. To find it we must journey within, to the uncharted territory which awaits our discovery.

The way to obtain spiritual truth directly is through the inner journey of soul. This individual process relies on no outside sources and is unique to each practitioner. Soul is our true identity, and only by activating its divine energies can absolute truth be known and brought into daily experience. The divine union we fervently seek comes via the awakening of the latent Sound within. The Masters of Light and Sound desire to lead those who want to go home through self-realization and God realization. To serve such souls is the Masters' entire mission and purpose. They stand, as always, waiting to welcome those who search, yearn, and weep for something more. The purpose of the light is to reveal our own entrapment; the transcendency of Sound lies in its power to free the ensnared soul.

CHAPTER 7

THE MEANING OF
THE SECOND COMING

Fortunate are those souls who never quite fit comfortably into life, who sense from their youth that there must be a Divine reason for this ferris wheel of existence. Their search for truth through life waxes and matures to an inner yearning for love, understanding, tranquility, and peace—for spiritual consciousness. Salvation is the target of their desire and the inner theme of their existence.

All seekers of truth yearn for spiritual consciousness. They realize that human consciousness is useful for opening doors, buying doughnuts, or spending a day at the beach; but these seekers desire more from life than do ordinary men or women. So salvation becomes the goal of these spiritual aspirants, and they begin to devote much time and effort in its pursuit.

Human consciousness alone is so polluted, limited, and unsatisfactory in fulfilling humankind's spiritual needs that nearly all realize some type of salvation is desperately needed. The idea of salvation permeates every religion, most cultures, all metaphysical paths, and the Light and Sound teachings as well. Of course, salvation is defined differently by different systems, paths, peoples, and religions, according to each viewpoint and level of consciousness. How do we recognize and actualize salvation as it relates to "the second coming"?

The transformative ideal of the second coming has existed and been anticipated for ages and ages. Generally in the Christian world, the second coming refers to the return of Jesus to Earth. However, the concept of the second coming far predates Jesus and Christianity, and stretches beyond to include societies worldwide. Even today, people in many lands eagerly await the return of their saviors or ancient gods and goddesses, and connect their personal salvation to this anticipated event.

> *As it stands, America is embarrassingly bankrupt in true spirituality. Instead of religion being "ONE," it has become many. Humankind is yearning for the simple truth of truths, but where is one to turn? The devoted have placed their hope and refuge in the coming of the Savior, the Messiah. All of earth's inhabitants ardently wish for the return of the Godman. The Hopis are searching for the other "Half of the Tablet"; Buddhists are awaiting the arrival of the "Matreya"; Christians look skyward for their "Second-Coming of Christ"; Eastern paths yearn for the "Avatar"; and Masons await the "Lost Word."*
>
> Sri Gary Olsen
> 1948 –
> Author and Master of Light and Sound

The Religious Viewpoint of the Second Coming

> *The coming of the Son of Man will be evident*
> *because the coming of the Son of Man will be like lightning*
> *striking in the East and flashing far into the West.*
> *Immediately after the distress of those days,*
> *the Sun will be darkened,*
> *the Moon will lose its brightness,*
> *the stars will fall from the sky,*
> *And then the sign of the Son of Man*
> *will appear in the heavens. (Matthew 24:27-30)*
>
> Jesus
> Master of Light and Sound

It is known that our true white brother, when he comes, will be all powerful and he will wear a red cap and a red cloak. He will be large in population and bring no other religion than his very own. He will bring with him the sacred stone tablets. Great will be his coming. None will be able to stand against him. With him will be two great ones.

Hopi elder, Thomas Banyacya
1909 –
Speaker for village chief Dan Katchongua
Village of Hotevilla, Independent Hopi Nation

In ancient times, so long ago that our cellular memory strains even to conceive of it, humankind's first god was the sun. Although the sun rose and shone faithfully every day, each eclipse brought fear that it would never return. The universal legend of a disappearing deity who promises to return when human need is at its zenith is rooted in the deep-seated fears of our collective consciousness with its primitive memories still intact. The promise of the second coming and the returning savior is deeply rooted within the human consciousness as well, and nearly all religions have incorporated it into their theology.

The concept of the resurrected savior existed in the Middle East thousands of years before the birth of Jesus. Zarathustra, the great emperor-god of Persia, was sacrificed and resurrected so that humankind could leave behind its tarnished state and return to its original purity. In ancient Egypt, the cult of Osiris and Isis held that Osiris was a wise ruler who resurrected as a godman after his jealous brother, Seth, sliced him to bits; and Isis, sister and wife of Osiris, reconstructed Osiris's body. Osiris lived on in divine fashion and became the god of the dead who judged humans' souls.

The story of gods being sacrificed so that humankind may live is also found in Babylon and ancient Sumeria, more than 2000 years before the time of Jesus. In the Babylonian poem of creation, the "Cosmology of Assur," the great god is sacrificed; and humankind is fashioned out of his blood. Who can say to what degree fact, myth, and symbology comprise these ancient tales? It is clear that many cultures have had and still have the myth of the sacrifice of a god or a man/god who was resurrected and is expected to return.

In the Americas, this belief has existed among the Hopi, the Incas, the Mayas, the Aztecs, and many lesser-known tribes for thousands of years. According to myth, Quetzalcóatl, the king-sage associated with the plumed serpent, descended into the underworld and cast himself into the fires to be transformed into the sun. His return to right the wrongs of man and to re-establish life within the true spiritual principles is eagerly anticipated by many throughout Mexico and Central and South America.

In North America, the Hopi legend of the return of Pahana is once again a story of a long-awaited second coming. According to the Hopi, we are now in the "fourth world." Similar Maya, Aztec, and Inca prophecies all concur that God has made the world uninhabitable at least three times when people departed from their innate spiritual center and became channels for the negativity of human consciousness.

Pahana, the "white brother," is one of a pair of twins who were entrusted with overseeing the Hopi world and making sure it existed in balance, with proper adherence to spiritual principles. Pahana left to observe other peoples and took with him part of the ancient stone tablet which had been entrusted to the Hopi by Maasauu, the god of the earth. The Hopi believe that Pahana will return with the missing part of the tablet during a time of great need. His power will be great; and he will restore balance and harmony, not only to the Hopi, but to the entire world as well.

Many Buddhist and Hindu sects also await the return of their cherished avatars to lead the followers from the darkness to the light. Traditional Hinduism recognizes four great cycles of time, which stretch into millions of years. At the end of each grand cycle, when humankind is steeped in materialism and hedonism, and the absence of godliness is at its zenith, the worlds are destroyed. After a period of rest, the worlds are recreated and a new "golden age" akin to a second coming and defined by peace, harmony among peoples, and attunement to God and spiritual laws, begins. Although many Eastern religions do not accept the notion of their saints, prophets, and teachers returning in exactly the same physical body with the same mannerisms and personality of their previous incarnations intact, they do accept the second coming. In fact, many believe that their saviors constantly reincarnate among them in a new body, yet bearing the same message.

In Judaism, the ancient God of the tribes of Israel is expected to manifest on earth as the promised messiah. The Christian perspective of the second coming is that the negative forces, represented by Satan, are said to be on the ascendant at the time the second coming draws near. The four horsemen of the apocalypse will be released and descend into the world, spreading war, famine, pestilence, and death. Christians will be persecuted and chaos will be the order of the day. At that point, the powers of Satan will reside in a human form, known as the anti-Christ who brings about a false utopia. Usually he is interpreted as an evil world ruler who will bear "the mark of the Beast." Relative peace will be established for a short time, and political and economic problems will have the appearance of being solved or under control.

The peace will be short-lived, and the period of time known as the Tribulation will continue. The earth is to be visited by seven angels bearing seven deadly plagues. Among the prophecies are an increase of the sun's heat, drying up of great rivers, terrible earthquakes, and massive tidal waves and flooding. Then the forces of the anti-Christ and the army of warrior angels amassed by God are to meet for the final battle between good and evil—Armageddon. In the midst of the great battle, Jesus the Christ is expected to return to earth and personally ensure the defeat of the anti-Christ and the forces of evil. Then the long-awaited thousand years of peace on earth can begin, for the devil will be chained and cast into the abyss; and a new, godly, social and political order will be established as the Messianic Age opens.

However, according to Revelation, *Satan shall be loosed out of his prison and shall go out to deceive the nations. (Revelation 20:7-8).* One more battle will remain as Jesus is urged by Ezekiel: *Son of Man, set thy face against Gog, the land of Magog. (Ezekiel 38:2).* This decisive battle will destroy the forces of evil, once and for all, and will close with the Judgment Day. *And I saw the dead, small and great, stand before God; ... and the dead were judged. (Revelation 20:12).*

Utopia will finally arrive on earth as "New Jerusalem," adorned with walls and streets of gold, gates of pearl, and foundations of many precious gems. *There is no need of the sun or the moon to shine on it, for the glory of God shines on it, and the Lamb is its lamp. (Revelation 21:23).* Thus, in this prophecy the faithful are to be rewarded with eternal life at the side of God. This viewpoint anticipates an external event within the framework of time and space.

This universal archetype reflects humankind's cry for a savior, who is both a god and a man, to return to repel the negative forces which humankind has allowed to run amuck within its collective consciousness, creating a world of disorder, deceit, and spiritual dishonor. The messiah is to bring salvation to a world of chaos, and in many religious interpretations, to a people unable to save themselves.

Such salvation requires faith, hope, and belief; it rests on the premise that God is infinitely merciful and compassionate, and that salvation can be obtained only through some external saving grace. This viewpoint also suggests that God the Creator was not impressive enough in Its splendid creation: that humankind is either too dull to perceive divinity within God's creation, or the Nameless One simply has failed to transfer the divine stamp of glory upon it. Apparently the spirit, or the Holy Ghost, also failed. Either it is too weak to reach humanity with its love, wisdom, and grace; or humankind is simply too disinterested or preoccupied to be alert to its subtle nudges. Therefore, the remaining element of the Holy Trinity, the Son of God, is sent to make a definitive personal appearance, which cannot fail to get our attention.

Ironically, this need for an external savior is contrary to the very faith, hope, and belief which sustains the concept to begin with. If we had true faith and true belief, would a messiah need to appear to work miracles in our midst? No, for true faith—based on genuine personal experience—leads beyond belief and into knowingness. The certainty of genuine spiritual experience brings us closer to the Divine and harmonizes us with the spiritual laws and principles. If authentic faith and belief are based on personal experience, the negative conditions which the savior comes to reverse would not exist.

The religious interpretation of the second coming, based largely upon the fears and needs of the human consciousness, is an external phenomenon centered upon redemption at the hands of a god of time, space, and separate human form. And just as no two story-tellers spin exactly the same tale, no two listeners hear exactly the same story.

The New Age Viewpoint of the Second Coming

Glowing expectations of a millennial all-spiritual Aquarian Age appear naive and unrealistic, unless they be limited to relatively isolated sections of mankind; and such an isolation would require at first some kind of world catastrophe and a much smaller world population.

Dane Rudhyar
1895 – 1985
Author, philosopher, astrologer

The New Age viewpoint of the second coming is largely a meta-physical perspective which stresses the idea of physical and spiritual evolution occurring within varying cycles of time. According to its proponents, the New Age itself is a metaphor for the second coming of the Christ Consciousness. This guiding light of a particular time represents the culmination of several major cycles of spiritual evolution and the birth of a new cycle or new age. Depending on which group one listens to, these cycles of time, which are ending in the present and forthcoming decade, are rooted in astrology; in Egyptian, Maya, Hopi, Inca, Aztec, Tibetan, or Hindu calendars or cosmology; or in the cycle of time and events written in the Bible itself.

Regardless of the sources drawn upon to support the contention that the New Age has dawned, most practitioners agree that the time is now. Although many New Age groups have varied points of view and agendas regarding the content and events of the second coming, there is a thread of similarity which can be traced through the diverse expectations of the loosely knit groups of New Age followers.

Most New Age philosophy agrees that the dawning of the Aquarian Age (anywhere from 1948 to 1997) marks the beginning of a new cycle of time, in which peace and harmony will eventually be restored to a troubled world. The 1990's are generally expected to be a period of turmoil when the established political, social, economic, and religious systems and institutions will be challenged by the New Age ideas of lifestyle and social structure. Astrologers pointed to the fact that during the years 1989-91, Pluto was within Neptune's orbit; and six planets repeatedly occupied the sign of Capricorn. Pluto is said to be the planet of cosmic transformation, and the grouping of six planets in one sign is a phenomenon which occurs only once in several hundred years.

Dire predictions abound regarding the changes that a higher level of vibration or spiritual awareness spawning the New Age will bring, as the forces of the new clash with the established consciousness and institutions of the old in our world. Many predict the earth itself will undergo drastic upheavals, including large changes in wind currents, the rising and falling of sea levels, the earth collapsing in many areas, and earthquakes and volcanic activity in destructive abundance. Yet this is only the beginning. Some New Age prognosticators predict a shift of the earth's axis, bringing massive tidal waves and flooding; seasons changing abruptly; and tremendous winds blowing across the face of the earth, killing millions and perhaps billions. Other New Age advocates believe that some type of increased destructive activity will be visited upon the earth, but that the shift of the earth on its axis probably will not occur.

To many New Agers, the period of the "tribulation," that time of grievous troubles and plagues, will be political more than environmental, with governments changing rapidly in all parts of the world as dictators and repressive states are replaced with more enlightened political systems. Such change will extract a price, leading to war and violent revolutions. Other New Age thinkers believe the approaching hard times will be a result of a massive collapse of the world economy and worldwide depression that will make the economic collapse of the 1930's look like the prosperity of the 1920's. Whatever form the tribulation supposedly takes, the New Age interpretation is that it certainly will occur.

We can see similarities between these New Age viewpoints and the views of many religious groups regarding a second coming. Both the metaphysical and the religious theories say that the stage must be set—the savior will only return when times are at their worst and when humanity is in its greatest need of salvation. The

New Age and religious perspectives part company, though, when specifying how this will occur. To most New Agers, the Battle of Armageddon is not a war between two armies; rather it is a battle between good and evil within one's own consciousness and within world societies at large. It is an ongoing attempt to create a healthier, more enriching environment and culture, both without and within, and the battlefield is within the human consciousness as well as in the political, economic, social, and environmental arenas. The success of this noble and worthy goal could only uplift the consciousness of the individual "warriors" and the planetary consciousness.

Most New Agers recognize that soul is our true nature, and that it represents original purity. Therefore, the second coming is seen as humanity's return to a higher spiritual level, closer to the nature of soul and the God within. If the great Battle of Armageddon is symbolically interpreted as a war between good and evil within the human consciousness, then the second coming can easily be seen as the emergence of the victorious forces of higher awareness; not necessarily the return of any particular godman, it is a rebirth in consciousness to a higher level of spirituality.

Another thread within New Age prophecies includes the possibility of the arrival of advanced civilizations from outer space. Many UFO watchers and advocates believe that helpers from Venus, Sirius, or the Pleiades will arrive on earth during the worst moments of the tribulation period and remove many earthlings to a place of shelter until the earth can be reinhabited.

From the New Age perspective, the true purpose of the second coming revolves around a relatively small number of people who are experiencing a new, higher level of consciousness and applying it to the world in which they live. This growing awareness is expected to usher in an age of peace, harmony, and prosperity on earth. Many New Agers harbor utopian visions—a contemporary version of New Jerusalem where we are all one, all brothers and sisters together.

Many proponents of New Age thought are expecting the thousand years of peace and harmony to be drastically different from our world today. Many expect a shift in consciousness or awareness where individuals are uplifted and transformed by the greater light

of the Christ, Pahana, Quetzalcóatl,or whatever savior consciousness is seen as ushering in the New Age. The boundaries between
the tribulation, the second coming, the Battle of Armageddon, and
the millennium are not as well defined as in Christian theology.
Some believe that we are in the time of the second coming now,
pointing to AIDS, famines in Africa and other areas, and worldwide drug addiction and drug wars as being a part of the plagues
predicted throughout the period of the tribulation. Yet they still
believe that the expected increase in awareness will be powerful
enough to transform the world into a veritable Garden of Eden.

Will the ancient Maya, Aztec, Hopi, and Inca prophecies of the
emergence of the enlightened world come true? The New Age
philosophers are well aware of ancient legends of Atlantis, Lemuria,
and the prehistoric misty past of Tibet that tell of a time when people lived in a golden age. Many fully expect the Golden Age to be
reincarnated shortly.

How the Masters of Light and Sound Regard
the Second Coming

> O pilgrims for the shrine! Where go ye? Where?
> Come back! Come back! For the Beloved is here!
> His presence all your neighborhood doth bless!
> Why will ye wander in the wilderness!
> Ye who are seeking God! Yourselves are He!
> Ye need not search! He is ye verily!

> Shamas-i-Tabriz
> 13th century Persian saint
> Master of Light and Sound

> A customer for God alone
>   obtains the Jewel through meditation;
> Opening the inner eye,
>   he beholds the treasure of liberation.

> The Adi Granth
> Compiled teachings of the Sikh gurus

The Masters of Light and Sound also consider the second coming to be a sacred event, yet their viewpoint is quite different from the expectations discussed previously. The Masters proclaim that the world is never without a true, living Master; that the savior has never left and is ever present both inwardly and outwardly. The Merciful One always provides Its children with an outer, flesh and blood, recognizable form of Itself; although the faces may change, the Son of God always dwells among us. The legends of the returning God-man do not adequately reflect God's love for each soul.

The Master is not a savior and does not exist to wash away the sins of humankind and bring the masses to spiritual liberation merely to alleviate our self-created conditions. Salvation is a personal experience; it has nothing to do with "the elect," the righteous 144,000, the masses of true believers, or any particular group of people of any kind. The Master exists to teach, guide, direct, motivate, and assist those individuals who want to save themselves. He constantly teaches that he cannot do *for* the student what can only be done *through* the student.

Our responsibility is to provide a fertile atmosphere for the Master's seed of wisdom and love to grow. Salvation cannot be reduced to spiritual welfare. It is a partnership between us and the Master which relies on upholding our end of the bargain. The Master does not disappoint, make false promises, or breach his contract in any way. Any living Master of Light and Sound will openly tell you that he is not the truest form of the Master. His main purpose is to prepare us for meeting the inner form of the Master, known as the Radiant Form—the direct personification of the Audible Life Stream Itself that is timeless, omnipotent, omnipresent, and One with the Supreme Deity. The Inner Master knows no bounds of time or space, and can work with one student or a thousand students simultaneously. This transcendental form of the Master is the True Guru, the Savior, and the Messiah.

The outer Master only wishes for his students to raise their soul energies to the third-eye center. When the Radiant Form of the Inner Master meets the soul within the third eye of the seeker, this is the "Second Coming" of the Messiah. This second coming has nothing to do with events in the external world within the framework of time and space. This long-awaited fulfillment of the legends of antiquity occurs when an individual soul comes into contact with the Radiant Form of the transcendental entity, the Inner Master. This is the beginning of soul's merging with its own divine nature.

Soul, the Inner Master, and the God within are all woven of the same divine fabric, producing a garment of spiritual distinction with which the human level of consciousness cannot be adorned. For soul to experience the second coming, it must escape the confines and limitations of the human state of consciousness and rise to the third-eye center, where spiritual consciousness begins. The journey of soul is the path to salvation. Good works, faith, prayer, and hope are all elements of light; and light alone cannot bring us into union with the inner savior. The Master promises that he can do this—by awakening soul and the latent Sound Current.

The true second coming is a miracle in consciousness, and those who experience it are altered for all time. The transformative power of the slumbering Master within us all cannot be overstated or exaggerated, and can only be described vaguely. On soul's journey, no greater joy awaits the seeker than meeting the Master within. Since this revolutionary event is an internal, spiritual experience, seekers must come to it, not vice versa. First, we must find a true outer Master who can introduce us to the awaiting Inner Master. Then we must raise our soul energies from the lower chakras to the third eye.

At this time, the Radiant Form of the Master appears with soul as Its witness. This deeply moving and transcendental spiritual reality cannot be experienced in the external world. It is neither the property of any religion nor the conclusion of an overactive imagination. It is more real than most seekers can imagine, but there is no set time for its occurrence. The true second coming must be found and discovered within. It will not come by turning pages on the calendar of cosmic time, awaiting some expected day.

No prophecy can surround an event which never happens in the future but always within the moment. The joy and the challenge of the spiritual life lies in searching for, finding, and activating our own individual truth! Waiting upon the savior to come and find you and focusing on events in the world of time and space in order to experience truth are only illusions. The second coming does not come to us at all; we must go within to find it!

Although the viewpoints of the Masters of Light and Sound may be quite different from the religious or the New Age perspectives of the second coming, certain similarities do exist. For example, the students enter a period of tribulation before they can experience the second coming. One experiences the plagues of fear, anxiety, doubt, loneliness, inadequacy, anger, and many more lower states of consciousness before the spiritual consciousness is born. The true seeker's tribulation has nothing to do with prophecy, plagues, disease, or floods—it is a period of inner purification.

The New Age version of the second coming is contained within a largely external scenario. Although not as rigidly defined as most religious interpretations, it deals with cycles of time, physical events, and utopian societies. The changes and shifts in consciousness at the heart of the New Age interpretation are worthy goals indeed, yet limited. Even if greater awareness were visited upon many souls; even if "space brothers" arrived with new technologies and intelligences; and even if a millennium of peace and harmony occurred—are not these events still woefully shy of the great spiritual goals of self-realization and God realization? True seekers are much more serious about the divine journey of soul (following the Sound) than in creating utopian societies (following the light).

Again, salvation is an inner, personal, and individual experience; and as more souls experience the realities of self-realization and God realization, no doubt the world will become a better place in which to live. When we are more concerned with improving the conditions in which societies exist than we are with finding and actuating the God within, we have put the cart before the horse. Utopia on earth is a noble attempt at reform; and although these are worthwhile efforts, they are extremely limited in terms of their goals. Even a prison of diamond walls and golden bars remains a prison. As true seekers, we desire liberation. The inner sojourn of soul can deliver such liberation.

The appeal of the Garden of Eden is found within the psychic consciousness. Golden ages, the ideal of reform, and the lessening of human suffering are worthy goals. Yet the body will come and go, and so will the earth, like sand castles washing to the sea. Our true home is that which knows no death. Is it not wise to scrutinize more closely our materials of construction, rather than blindly building that which is destined to perish?

The Messiah exists for you, and exists within you. The Son of Man is closer to you than your own heartbeat. All the great masters, saviors, and avatars the world has ever known are no different from you in their essence. Cycles of time persist; truth exists. The time for truth is always now, and the place for the New Jerusalem is within you. The millennium can begin at the moment of your choosing.

Your second coming is always close at hand. How deeply do you desire it?

SECTION III

THE SPIRITUAL PROGRESSION

CHAPTER 8

WHO IS A SEEKER?

Now that the distinction between the spiritual energies of Light and Sound has been made, these energies, which are truly one in the higher sense, will be referred to collectively as Sound.

The first and foremost principle of the Sound is this:

Soul exists because God loves it.

Soul, created by God out of Its own essence, is perfect. It is never our state of grace that separates us from God realization—only our state of mind. With this understanding as a part of our spiritual armor, we easily can see that all love, all grace, and all purity reside within us as soul. Soul is the true self and our true nature. To begin to realize and release our divine potential, we must be able to imagine that soul exists within us, and to see that all the traits of a true seeker are ours to draw upon whenever we choose to acknowledge them. This spiritual truth is the promise of the Sound, and Sound is the essence that will enliven our spiritual dream!

Our motives matter supremely in negotiating the transition from need to devotion. Whatever ideas and situations bring a seeker to the path may seem important, but they are not critical. It is important to examine which traits serve to motivate and propel true spiritual seekers beyond anger, greed, distrust, and worldly desires, to an attitude where truth is sought for its beauty alone and because it is synonymous with the pure love of God. True spiritual seekers need no other motive for their search. Can those who want much but will trade little, or the distraught who seek only relief from their karma become devoted seekers who want only God's love and spiritual truth?

We all sometimes feel a twinge of guilt or embarrassment as we think about our motives in seeking spirituality. Who among us is so pure and noble that we cannot recognize some lesser motives and considerations within ourselves? If we lived in a state of spiritual perfection already, would we have any need to walk the spiritual path? Of course not. As spiritual seekers, we must recognize both sides of the duality—our positive traits as well as areas of limitations requiring improvement or fresh examination. We can, and in time must, accept them both in the same light; through accepting our limitations, soul and the Master can work together to overcome them.

All shortcomings and limitations are merely aberrations of the mind. In due time, given a sincere effort on our part, the illuminating body of soul can burn through the fog of doubt and confusion and reveal to those who ardently yearn for truth that they are never turned away. Why? Because the first great principle of Sound is, and always has been, that soul exists because God loves it.

Past Experiences Have Run Their Course

Every seeker's life reaches a time when past experiences have run their course, a point of "divine discontent" when they feel anxious, moody, restless, and ready to set out and explore new directions or chart a finer course. This inner tension is caused by the friction between our desires to expand spiritually and the opposing force within that wants to rest, recuperate, and postpone the new leg of the journey for a while. Although our experiences in life may have taught us much, restored our faith in God, and allowed us to trust in divine guidance, we come to feel that there must be more to the spiritual life. We feel unfulfilled and incapable of pouring any more energy into the current endeavor, be it a religion, a metaphysical path or study, or simply trying to unravel the mysteries of the Divine by our own devices. Outwardly, we may be relatively comfortable with our lots in life; we may have good friends, good mates, and satisfying jobs. Yet a gnawing tension exists within that we cannot quite describe. We only know that our happiness is incomplete and that there must be more to life, especially our spiritual life.

This divine discontent—disillusionment with what the world has to offer as substitutes for knowing the Divine within—is an enviable position as well as a painful one. From this position, seekers sometimes look with scorn at those who truly are content with their places in life's drama, while secretly envying their contentment. At the same time, we realize that the things which bring contentment to others' lives are not sufficient balm for our own heartfelt pain. All seekers must make a decision here because spirit, which guides and rules us all, has led each of us to a situation where we have the awesome opportunity to either continue the search for truth or somehow come to terms with this unhappiness and heartfelt restlessness.

Many true seekers find themselves in such a position, filled with their prior understanding of the relationship between human and Divine, but unfulfilled and yearning to experience more. Actually, divine discontent is really a wonderful ploy of spirit to aid in our spiritual growth or unfoldment. Now the opportunity exists to make the dream real! Just as many of us avoid seeing a doctor or dentist until our pain becomes unbearable, many times we avoid making a real commitment to a new endeavor until our discontent and inner turmoil have reached a crisis point.

The mind serves as a great tool when infused by soul, but it is a poor master. Therefore we must learn to still the mind. Even the most sincere seekers are still ruled largely by their minds and their emotions. Changes, transitions, and spiritual unfoldment always involve letting go of old ways to make way for new. The mind usually resents any changes in point of view and resists them; it feels it already has all the answers and the correct points of view, although its curiosity is insatiable. Although we have spiritual feelings, thoughts, and intuition, until we become self-realized the Sound is inactive and soul is at rest. The mind and the emotions with all their likes and dislikes, desires and attachments, beauty and defilements, and senses of identity are what cause us to behave as we do.

Many factors bring us to see that our past experiences with the spiritual life have run their course. Commonly, we become dissatisfied with the level of truth that is revealed from external sources, particularly from religious institutions. However, as seekers, we face great danger when our frustrations with organized religion lead us to "throw out the baby with the bath water," and make us drop the whole idea of attempting to find truth. But the spiritual journey should always be one of excitement and the joy of discovery! When a particular path or religion ceases to move us deeply, it is a time for rejoicing, not despair. When the past experiences have run their course, a new opportunity for meeting the Divine within awaits the seeker who is ready.

Our past experiences have run their course when we become disenchanted with group prayer, group social functions within the church, and all other forms of group salvation and group identification. We can then see how the individual soul has become secondary to group consciousness, and how group mentality has become a conduit from which flows its moral code, its prejudices, and its self-righteousness. Any attempt to diverge from the group's point of view may result in our being labeled anything from a misfit to a heretic.

The group aspect of religion relies on safety in numbers for its power, and uses fear and censure to wield that power. Promises of salvation through religion almost always require adherence to the prevailing group mentality. Nothing could be further from the truth. Salvation was, is, and always will be a personal spiritual experience—never the particular possession of any race, nationality, or creed. So another trait of truth seekers is their desire to be free from all such restrictive ideas and associations. Salvation comes from two sources—the grace of the Lord, and the willingness of the seeker to make a strong personal effort. Self-realization and God realization are the twin goals of the Sound. "Group realization" does not exist.

When we become disenchanted with the group mentality of the various religions and come to believe that real truth can only be found within, then our past experiences with religion have run their course. We may be depressed, down-and-out, and seeking solace from our misery by escaping into drugs, alcohol, or other obsessive behaviors, suspended between our past experiences with seeking truth and newer, still unknown adventures.

Transcending the religious concept of seeking truth to enter into a spiritual approach involves the seeker's eventual dissatisfaction with morals as the guideline to determine good or bad. Morals are defined by a majority of a given society, and what that society deems to be the correct point of view or mode of behavior usually grows out of prevailing religious beliefs. Certain modes of dress, sexual behavior, and lifestyle are deemed to be acceptable, and even good, while other points of view and ways of expression are bad, even sinful. Morals change from time to time and place to place, serving as an external guide for those who have not yet been able to go within to find truth. This can be a particularly searing point for many seekers to deal with, especially in the United States, which was founded on and remains based in the Puritan ethic.

Morals exist to keep societies functioning and to provide us with some sort of civilized environment in which to unfold as spiritual beings. We grow up and become socialized into the prevailing "vibe of the tribe," adopting those morals that pervade our society through the media, the government, the educational system, the church, the community, the family, and many other more subtle ways. This conditioning flows freely into the subconscious mind, affecting our mental and emotional makeup. Our actions and behaviors become more and more mechanical as habits are formed, solidified, and constantly reinforced by the external world. Slowly but surely, the light in the eye of the young child grows dimmer and dimmer as soul becomes increasingly veiled by the overwhelming influences of the world, its customs, and its laws.

The Masters of Sound do not advocate anarchy. However, seekers discover that soul, which lies within, is the truest and highest source of ethical conduct. A middle road exists between the rigid, external moralism we encounter in churches and in society, and the *laissez-faire,* "do your own thing" attitude that denies others their freedoms and can even endanger lives. This road of self-determination puts the responsibility of determining and implementing one's own ethics squarely on the seeker's shoulders.

All great Masters unequivocally state, as Jesus taught: *The Kingdom of Heaven is within.* When seekers become aware of divine discontent, the next step to continue to grow calls for a complete change of method—realizing that the external world, learned people, pilgrimages, and holy scripture can never provide union with the Divine. Because God isn't in the external world, we must go within to find truth.

When we change our methods of inquiry into realizing truth, we come to see that the external search is based on faith. Others tell us what truth is, and we are asked to have faith that its revelators, such as the priestcraft, are correct. Faith invokes the feeling or emotional element within us, providing the necessary energy and impetus to enliven our spiritual search and make it real. This vitalizing force is of great value and cannot be overlooked, but faith does not have the sustaining power we're seeking. Once the value of faith has been incorporated into the seeker's being, then it can be replaced by a deep desire to *know* and *experience* inner spiritual unfoldment.

The Masters of Sound teach that the search for truth is internal, and that *we* hold the searchlight. Only when soul has been restored to its proper place of rulership in our own constitution can truth be revealed, because soul is truth and the essence of God Itself. Soul can know, be, and see truth instantly, with no outward search or journey required.

Going within is a simple process of focusing one's attention on the third eye to penetrate the layers of emotion and mind (including the subconscious) which surround soul and make it a prisoner in its own home. Contemplating this way for a brief period of time each day, with the third eye as the focal point, returns our energies (which are scattered throughout the body and out into the external world) to this third eye. This spiritual process can be developed in a relatively short period of time.

Truth seekers make a strong, constant effort to reveal and examine their behavior to see what steps are necessary to break down their conditioned responses to life. For example, we grow up being taught we need eight hours of sleep a night, and we have abided by that dictum for years. But is it really good or healthy? Spiritual seekers faced with such a question experiment to see what is good for them, as individuals. Once the body aligns itself to this pattern, six hours a night might leave many more rested, alert, and energetic for the coming day. But how will we ever come to know this unless we question the assumptions of our upbringing and society?

No book, holy scripture, family teaching, or social morals will do it for us; we must determine for ourselves, by contemplating the questions that arise, what our own course of spiritual action may be. We have no outside structure to support our decisions, nor anyone on whom to cast blame should our decisions lead us astray. We alone are responsible for our creations. This particular point of spiritual maturity is often a stumbling block for seekers. It is rather easy to become dissatisfied with tight-lipped moralism; it's not quite so easy to be willing to go within and attempt to learn what type of action will foster the necessary experiences needed for continued spiritual unfoldment.

Questioning morals affects all areas of experience. Truth seekers consider nothing to be true unless they have experienced it, while remaining open and willing to view all outside authority objectively. They know there is no way to discover truth except by going within and listening to the small, subtle urges through which soul and the Inner Master speak. Masters of Sound teach no dogma. Their sole purpose is to return the power, authority, and freedom of choice to weary souls who are tired of being manipulated by the world and its ways. The journey homeward never leads outward; it always leads inward. There is no other way to directly experience truth.

Often, when we make a break with the past, we rebel against it in some way. How much better it is to accept the past for what it has been; to be thankful for the learning experiences it has brought then to dive headlong, willingly and confidently, into the present moment. But how many of us are so pure? Don't be surprised to see other, less pure reactions taking place within your consciousness; and try not to be too disturbed by it when you see it.

When confronted by our own negative behaviors, we can easily slip into self-pity or, worse yet, self-hatred. Caught in duality, we feel ourselves to be spiritually oriented individuals on one hand; and on the other hand, we see ourselves in negative ways—being overly fearful or skeptical about the future and angry, dismayed, or disillusioned about the past. As our self-esteem drops, we can easily lose sight of our spiritual natures and identify only with our negative traits and behaviors. At this critical point on our journey, we can easily become so disillusioned with the world and ourselves that we disqualify ourselves as seekers: "How can I be a seeker?... Look at me. I'm a mess. I'm not even a good human being!" Then, rather than try to stop this downward slide, we identify with it and define ourselves as failures, unfit for a spiritual life. Thus, we may set into motion a train of events which may take years, or even several lifetimes, to reverse. If we do this, we are playing right into the hands of the negative power. One moment of sincere reflection can reverse this tendency.

The negative power within us is here to test, delay, and stop our spiritual progress in any way possible, setting us up to identify with all our negative qualities and to feed them with our energies of thought and feeling. It urges us to focus on our limitations, our unworthiness, and our distrust; and to magnify them as we identify with them. Only constant awareness of this negative energy of mind can prevent our getting caught in its trap.

Expressing negative emotions and seeking to escape the dilemmas of a spiritual seeker do not in any way disqualify anyone from the path, so don't let the negative power within you get such a grip that you disqualify yourself. A certain amount of frustration, fear, anger, and other symptoms of one's "divine discontent" are probably going to occur—natural reactions of the mind and emotions to your spiritual journey up to this point. The hallmark of truth seekers is freedom from both self-censure and overt indulgence in these passions of the mind and emotions, and sincere efforts at self-control and moderation.

Truth seekers realize that at the heart of our nature, we are soul and one with the Divine. Coming to see life and our own experiences from this position creates great changes. The negative force begins losing its power when we no longer choose to feed it with our own energies of thought and feeling. By seeing ourselves as essentially soul, experiences in life become valuable lessons, gifts from the Divine; no longer do we bemoan our fate and our lot in life. We come to accept our experiences without classifying them as good or bad, positive or negative, but rather as opportunities for further spiritual unfoldment.

Willingness to Assess and Release the Past

Many seekers who recognize that their past experiences with religion, metaphysics, or other paths have run their course—that they have extracted all they can from them—still have mental and emotional ties to the teachings of their past. This attachment is quite natural, and expected. However, these ties limit many seekers to their previous studies or attitudes on life in a way that prevents them from experiencing what the Sound has to offer.

Jesus was a great spiritual master and teacher, but certainly not the only one—so were Buddha, Krishna, Kabir, Nanak, and many, many others. In fact, several living masters may coexist in one period of time. Still, some seekers can accept a Master of Sound, but only as a master who is working under Jesus, or only as a subordinate of Buddha or Krishna. Still others see the Master as a New Age messiah sent from Venus or the Pleiades to usher in the Aquarian Age. A few are perfectly willing to accept the teachings and principles of Sound, but not accept a Master at all. These seekers have not yet released the binding mental and emotional ties to their past experiences, many of which were negative, and may even have involved being manipulated by pseudo-gurus.

We tend to become fixated on a particular point or level of truth, and surround it with all our thoughts and emotional feelings. Then, rather than viewing truth as a river, which always has a new vista around the next bend, we see it as a lake—more or less the same everyday, serene and calming, and even bringing a relative degree of security. However, its permanent, fixed boundaries allow no room for change or unfoldment; and our minds become attached to the familiar view of reality or truth. Rather than being willing to assess and release the past, we hold it fast. Nothing can be more dangerous for the seeker.

Two key attitudes create the ability and willingness to assess and release the past. First, we start to view our past as experience, understand our old binding emotional and mental ties to it, and then release our identifications with the experience. Second, we practice seeing the beauty and perfection in our experiences and relate to them as valuable spiritual training or learning experiences. When we develop the ability of seeing all our life situations, both past and present, as necessary for spiritual learning, then we will have a much easier time of detaching our feelings from them and moving on to our next step.

Something quite marvelous happens at this point of the spiritual journey—we begin to see truth as it really is, undiluted by our judgments or our feelings—the way soul sees truth. The mind and the emotions only see and feel according to their conditioned responses; soul sees what really is. As we learn to perceive the big picture, the viewpoint of soul, we begin to recognize the lessons involved in all our experiences, and the beauty of the spiritual journey to this point becomes apparent. This beauty is so overwhelming and so perfect that we easily transcend our petty opinions about what previously seemed so good or bad in our past experiences.

Releasing our opinions and emotional ties to our past grows out of being able to properly assess them. This comes from being able to see the whole, rather than focusing on the parts, which springs from our willingness to grow and unfold spiritually. If we really are willing to attempt to see truth, it will not be hidden from us. If we feel safe, secure, and happy with our cherished feelings and opinions about life, then the mind and emotions are winning the battle, and soul's emergence remains stifled and delayed.

Our willingness to assess and release past ideas about the spiritual life also concerns our ties to the external world. Many seekers have assessed and released their previous ideas from numerous areas of psychic consciousness. After receiving valuable insight and information from various studies, they have come to see their limitations, and seek a new avenue of finding greater truth. Yet how much of our focus continues to be outer directed? Indeed, the biggest trap we may encounter on soul's journey is seeking happiness and truth through the external world as we search endlessly for the right car, job, or lover, the right place to live, or the ideal vacation. The happiness and well-being of our friends, family, and children dominate our attention. Don't we use these activities merely to seek happiness and fulfillment in the external world? External happiness vacillates from day to day, hour to hour, and moment to moment. What we were content with yesterday is not quite enough for today. Our happiness is replaced by pain and anxiety. How much time and energy remain for our spiritual pursuits?

This is not a condemnation of the external world nor the desire to be happy. This world is both a beautiful and an ugly place, and the desire to be happy and fulfilled is an inborn trait of soul. Seekers finding truth, happiness, and fulfillment within soul express it outwardly in love and joy. To pursue joy and fulfillment through an external means directly opposes the viewpoint of true seekers. Being happy, joyous, and free cannot result from whether or not you are liked, respected, or have put in a good day's work. What is it, then, that brings you happiness? Truth seekers are never completely happy, fulfilled, nor free until we have merged with our own divine essence, the God within.

True happiness and joy do exist; however, they only exist within. Soul is a joyful entity! It lives in a natural state of bliss, so it has no need of achieving happiness. Instead, it happily achieves. Soul does not allow the mind's paltry substitutes for happiness to replace its innate contentment. When seekers are willing to assess and release their previous goals and desires for the one great desire—to know their true, higher self—soul's journey home begins.

Willingness to Act on Your Own Behalf

Just as we go to school here in the physical to learn the ways of the world, we also "go to school" as soul. This classroom for soul's learning is much larger than any great university. Our parents, children, environments, talents, and weaknesses all serve as our teachers so that we can come to discover our higher, truer nature—our identity as soul. Soul's journey is far greater than any of us can even imagine. It encompasses many, many lifetimes and life forms, and has no end. Everyone is included—every plant, animal, rock, and atom—and all are part of the divine drama of unfoldment and the universal body of God. As we gain more insight into this great law and begin to implement it more and more in our lives, it becomes much easier to see that each of our experiences, situations, and problems has been a lesson in the school of life that we had to learn to continue unfolding.

Just being in the classroom doesn't guarantee any success for the student, or for the spiritual seeker. To be good students here in the physical world, we must pay attention. How can we expect to learn if we let our attention wander out the window, back to yesterday's ball game, or forward to tonight's date? The same is true in our spiritual lives—our attention is a critical factor. As seekers, part of our willingness to act on our own behalf is striving to see beyond the humdrum and routine of daily life and putting our attention on the spiritual learning being presented.

Only the bold and adventuresome go forth on the path of Sound. The overriding spiritual principle here is simply this:

You must act to know.

Many times, in our laziness, we try to reverse this principle in hopes of gaining truth or enlightenment, thinking that we can wait until we know the truth and then act upon it. Seekers have many avenues and opportunities to act, to test and experiment, and to seek and find truth. They eventually act on their own behalf—even in the face of their unknowing, their doubt, and their skepticism. This attitude really isn't much more than applying the scientific method of inquiry to the spiritual aspect of life. Science is based on the principle that we must act to know. The physical workings of our planet and the universe are uncovered through experimentation, not revelation; and we approach the secrets of soul in the same manner.

Science, as well as the spiritual search, proceeds from a point of provisional faith. In science, researchers are continually willing to act, and if they find new levels of truth, to act again. Starting with a hunch, a feeling, or some evidence suggesting that something may be true, they design an experiment to test this hunch or hypothesis. If they find evidence that indicates their hypothesis may be true, they have new ground on which to form further hypotheses and experiments. This is provisional faith and experimentation rather than absolute faith and reliance on an outside source to provide truth without evidence. The "acting to know" asked of spiritual seekers is no more than provisional faith and experimentation. We are asked to accept nothing at face value, but rather to be willing to act, and provided we get results, to act again. What might the frog have found, had he been willing to hop outside his well with the swan?

Although the willingness to act on one's own behalf may seem quite elementary, it actually lies at the heart of the spiritual life. Nothing else can provide greater results. This willingness separates the would-be seeker from the true seeker and the beginner from the serious spiritual student, for without the willingness to act, seeking is more a mental study than a true spiritual quest.

All seekers who investigate any Sound path need some sort of proof or verification of the teachings and the Master. This is as it should be. However, many students seek the verification at a strictly mental level, wanting the teachings to be in harmony with their already established ideas about spiritual truth. Many seekers read a book or two, or listen to a talk, and when they find some discrepancy between what they presently believe to be true and what is being presented, they stop immediately and discontinue their investigation, not at all willing to act on their own behalf. They are more willing to seek comfort in ideas about reality than to discover reality itself. Truth seekers, when confronted with discrepancies between what they believe and what another says, do not instantly accept or reject the new input. They simply act in order to know; they experiment.

Suppose a spiritual seeker reads in the teachings of Sound that the negative power is the most powerful force in the four lower planes, and its job is to delay the seeker's spiritual progress at all costs. A seeker who believes our world to be highly positive and full of hope and opportunity may be shocked by the statement that the negative power is ruling our world, not having recognized the existence of the negative power or simply having chosen to ignore it. Yet if one is open minded and willing to research the point, one may form a test case and decide to do some critical self-examination to test the hypothesis: "If the negative power that seeks to delay my progress is so strong, then I should see much evidence of its existence in my thoughts, words, and deeds." One may attempt to "stand apart," as soul, and observe the workings of his or her own mind.

Over a period of time, such seekers may see an extremely powerful force within themselves that enjoys anger, thrives on lust, is overly vain and motivated by greed, and that forms strong emotional ties and attachments to possessions and its own self-serving ideas. Eventually they may even come to see this negative force as a great ally, one that allows them to expose their own lower nature so they may grow and unfold spiritually. Whatever they see, they have been willing to act on their own behalf, so they can come to know.

The spiritual journey of Sound is for individuals; it is not carried forward through group consensus or by relying on the opinions of others. Accepting any supposed truth without discovering it for yourself is just as dangerous as rejecting it without experimentation. A great guru of Sound once asked ten of her students how they knew that sugar was sweet. The first nine tasted the sugar and said that it was sweet. The tenth student said that the sugar was sweet without tasting it—it was common knowledge. The guru, pretending to be angry, shouted, "The proof is in your mouth, not in the sugar!"

Self-Discipline

We have the right to choose our own course of events, but our minds and emotions have a thousand concerns; and we continuously act according to our desires for comfort, pleasure, and well-being. Even inaction is a course of action. We often react to pain and discomfort—physical or emotional—by sending out some energy of action in thought, word, or deed. In a spiritual sense, disciplining our attention is the key to truly acting on our behalf.

Spiritual seekers attempt to continuously monitor their point of attention, for what we dwell on and give life to through thought is what we become. This is a life-long effort. We all are like radios in the sense that we are capable of tuning into a very large band of frequencies and then transmitting a particular frequency or vibration out into the world. We express self-discipline in how we control the tuning of our radio. This enables us to act on our own behalf and on behalf of our own higher self—soul.

For example, at night, Sarah sets her alarm for 6:30 A.M. She has a busy day ahead and wants to rise early enough to have time to do a spiritual exercise in the morning. The alarm rings at 6:30 A.M., waking her from a sound sleep. Upon waking, her mind is flooded with all sorts of images of the day to come: "What time do I have to be at work? When is my appointment downtown? How will my interview go at 4 P.M.? How will I dress today?" Just as quickly as the mind presents these questions, it reacts to them in thought and emotion, creating anxiety and tension as she becomes fearful of negative results: "Better get a little more sleep; I'll do my spiritual exercise later."

Sarah met her first experience of the day without using self-discipline to act on her own behalf. She chose to let her mind and emotions automatically react to the new day with fear and anxiety. She let her mind scatter her attention, dissecting the day into its parts—a meeting here, an appointment or interview there—as she reacted to all the upcoming activities of the day. Her energies immediately began flowing outwardly to the objects of her thoughts and concerns. Since her energies were all flowing outwardly, she suddenly felt tired again, so back to sleep she went. Very simply, Sarah failed to use any discipline in monitoring her attention and stumbled headlong into the trap of letting her mind and emotions usurp soul's viewpoint in determining her actions.

How could applying some discipline have changed this scenario? Let's start over again at 6:30 a.m. The alarm rings, and Sarah awakens. Once again, her mind goes to work and begins dissecting. "Stop!" Sarah is aware the new day has begun and immediately knows that discipline is the key to monitoring her attention so she can act on her own behalf, as soul. She centers her attention inwardly, at the third eye, and her energies immediately begin flowing inwardly to this point of attention. Seeing the upcoming day of challenges as fertile ground for further spiritual unfoldment—not only as part of her spiritual journey, but also from the viewpoint of the whole—she joyously welcomes it! She feels relaxed and at ease with herself, comfortable and content, and knows that deep within, as soul, she has nothing to fear in this world. She is aware that all her experiences in the day ahead are only for her spiritual betterment, so she can continue to recognize and realize her own true nature. With this attitude or viewpoint, she washes her face, brushes her teeth, and sits down to do her morning spiritual exercise.

True seekers work hard at monitoring their point of attention and do their best to learn from their failures, as well as successes. Of course, we face many moments during the day when our discipline will be challenged. The world is a cruel taskmaster indeed. In some of these moments when mind and emotions control us, we will fail, experiencing life from the point of view of the parts, rather than the whole—an old, familiar identification that we will work to rise above, again and again. This is nothing more than discipline, and as sincere students, we come to realize that this is the key to allowing ourselves to truly act in our own behalf. The potential for having a great, joyous, spiritual day or a humdrum, tension-ridden, migraine day are both present within the consciousness of the seeker. Discipline is more than half the battle, and true seekers remain constantly aware of this principle by consciously training ourselves to continuously monitor our point of view.

CHAPTER 9

AWAKENING TO THE SOUND WITHIN

The Masters of Sound promise to set us free. They state unequivocally that soul's journey through the many levels of consciousness within our bodies is the most exciting and most daring journey we could ever embark upon. This movement in consciousness is not for the faint of heart, yet it is for all humankind. This truth is for all, yet so few seem to have found it. The presence of a true living Master, coupled with the teachings of divine origin, create a spiritual potential that is as rare as it is supreme.

God's grand scheme and spiritual design has placed the royal road to spiritual riches within our own bodies. This paradox of spiritual reality is solved only when we come to know the content of our own minds. In the beginning of our journey, it is always the mind that separates us from truth. As the ego and the mind conspire against us, we still consider the mind to be our best friend, and our only hope for spiritual understanding. The ego supports the mind's belief that it is highly capable of discerning truth on its own, and both rebel at the suggestion that they have cleverly trapped themselves, and soul as well, within the confines of their own identities. Even in the present social atmosphere of self-help, few can admit how desperately they need guidance to find their own true self.

The contemporary New Age atmosphere focuses largely on human potential and endeavor. While its upbeat presentation of our inherent divinity and capabilities is laudable, its failure to address the enormity of humankind's illusion and self-delusion is a gross spiritual injustice. Until we come to see the scope of our dilemma in a realistic and honest way, we have little hope of escaping the web of illusion. We cannot afford to ignore the fact that we live in a world of untruth, and that we continually perpetuate its survival by paying homage and obeisance to our lower natures. Our identification with the mind, the ego, and the personality have put a stranglehold upon soul and our divine nature.

Our birthright is freedom, truth, love, and beauty. We are not born free, yet we are born to experience freedom. Soul knows no likes or dislikes. It is always content, regardless of circumstances. It has nothing to prove or to gain. It is complete within itself, yet it constantly nourishes all life. It lives through giving, not through acquisition. True spiritual freedom occurs when soul breaks loose from the shackles of the mind and the ego. Few souls experience such freedom from the chains of the mind and its incessant desires and opinions, yet there are many who have tasted this divine elixir before us, in this world and in many others.

The Wake-Up Call

What is this delusion in which we are adrift? We are the indweller of the man-body but have become identified with the body so much that we have become as if we were the body itself. This body has been given to you with the grace of God to find your way back to Him.

Kirpal Singh
1894 – 1974
Author, lecturer, former president of the
United Nations World Fellowship of Religions

*So long as the five enemies [anger, lust, greed, attachment, and
vanity] have control of the house, the soul is a helpless prisoner.
They leave it only when the owner means business and will toler-
ate their presence no longer.*
Maharaj Sardar Bahadur Jagat Singh
Author, lecturer
20th Century Master of Light and Sound

We sense when it's time for a change. The wake-up call has its
inner expression in a realization or a feeling that it is time to
expand spiritually. In such a mode of spiritual receptivity, we can
rest assured that what we need is not far away. As we desire to
explore and encounter the higher levels of consciousness which lie
dormant within, this inward, blessed desire often leads us to a way
of life that can help define and give form to that which we perceive
within. To the very fortunate, the wake-up call leads to a true Master.

When we find ourselves at the trailhead of soul's journey, we
usually feel as though we have been seeking truth all our lives, yet
somehow its ethereal nature has eluded us, and we may have even
thrown up our hands and exclaimed, "Que sera, sera!"—whatever
will be, will be. As we mature in our spiritual search and we come
to realize that truth is within, this leads us to the new experiences
which are necessary for continued unfoldment. We now seek in a
less frantic, though more active way, and this attitude, coupled with
a strong dose of recognition, is good preparation for continued
searching and discovery. Still, until the urge for truth is genuinely
fulfilled, we remain discontent.

Of course, our efforts and even our worst mistakes are never in
vain. As our experiences with the spiritual life grow, we discover
much of value and discard many limited truths. This discontent can
lead us to fulfill our yearning for the Divine with substitutes, rang-
ing from drugs, alcohol abuse, or uncontrolled sexual activity to
milder, equally entrapping activities—pursuing wealth, academic
standing, security, or a fulfilling marriage or career. Although there
is no inherent right or wrong in any of these activities, the trap is
that they may become permanent substitutions for the desire for
truth. These activities can be vehicles for experiences which will
help us find truth, but should never be viewed as truth, in and of
themselves. In fact, truth does not exist in the outside world, or in

any of its pursuits.

Truth can be found within soul. As our awareness of this simple spiritual fact expands, we begin to leave outward seeking behind and move into subtle alignment with the will of the Divine. We still search for truth and greater spiritual realities, but now our attention turns inward. This is the first stage of the seeker's wake-up call. We still may actively pursue substitutes for God, but in our hearts we know it is to no avail. When we experience rejection by, and for, the outer world, yet still long for truth, truth is likely close at hand. Only our earnest, deep longing and actual need for truth brings us the opportunity to experience it. Those who are content with their present level of consciousness or awareness have no need for the wake-up call. Only the truth seeker has.

Divine discontent (disillusionment with what the world offers as a substitute for the Divine within) is a necessary prerequisite in the higher education of all seekers. It can express itself with strong feelings or subtle realizations. It can entrap us in our misguided reaction to discontent, or set us free. Divine discontent does not mean an utter rejection of the world and its ways, nor that a nice house, a useful career, or a loving family and friends are evil or negative in any way. It is not an end, in and of itself, but a means to an end. As spiritual consciousness ascends and gradually replaces the hectic desires of human consciousness, all our familiar institutions of human life take on greater, not lesser, meaning.

Divine discontent allows us to step back from what we have believed is true and examine it in a stronger, broader, more illuminating light. This is our escape from the clutches of illusion that grasp us so firmly and tightly. A new awareness that all genuine truth can only be found within replaces our previously held illusion that the world can make us truly happy and set us free.

There is no such thing as spiritual growth; we only continually become more deeply aware of what already lies within. As this new level of awareness takes hold within our spiritual vitals, the true seeker's heartfelt desire and soul-inspired need for greater spiritual understanding brings newer, deeper levels of truth, and contact with soul. The Masters of Sound describe this process as "unfold-ment" or "awakening." This divinely inspired wake-up call cannot easily be ignored. It is extremely difficult to remain asleep when our higher selves desire to wake up. The buzzer rings, and we are advised, in the words of Jesus, *When you put your hands to the plow-share, give no thought to turning back. (Luke 10:62).* The divine alarm clock seems to have no snooze button.

The nature and content of the wake-up call varies from person to person. Some seekers experience a rush of energy as new spiritu-al inflows begin to rearrange their states of consciousness and their thoughts and feelings. Other seekers, although very much aware and appreciative of the new spiritual impetus, experience long periods of tiredness and drowsiness. When seekers are sincere, they need not be too concerned with how the wake-up call affects them. They will care little about external effects and will be highly appre-ciative of the movement in awareness and consciousness which their new experience brings. This appreciation is enough; it breeds true sincerity within, allowing for understanding and acceptance of external reflections.

Many times, when we are in the midst of exploring potentially new aspects of truth, our rates of change accelerate rapidly. As our spiritual life pulse quickens and we find the synchronicities in our lives multiplying, our psychic as well as our spiritual awarenesses arise: we know who is on the phone before we answer it; we think of other people and suddenly they stop by; we ask for guidance inwardly, and the answers manifest—perhaps through a book we have found or a dream. When the Divine within us sets the wheels of truth in motion, we never lack for miracles in our lives.

When our spiritual desires are peaking and openness to truth is our greatest motivator, the Master is not very far away. Soul is slumbering; the wake-up call signals an opportunity for new life. If you are so fortunate as to find a true Master, rise quickly, splash some water on your face, and follow. You may rise and retire every day, but soul will never slumber again.

The Awakening Process

The whole creation is engaged in feverish and senseless pursuits. It suffers dismay and disappointment at every step. We shed plenty of tears for money, wife and children, and suffer agony and anguish through loss of them. But if we were to weep earnestly for God for only one day, we would surely attain Him.

Maharaj Sardar Bahadur Jagat Singh
Author, lecturer
20th century Master of Light and Sound

The Audible Life Stream exists to give you spiritual freedom from the clutches of illusion. Over eons, the Masters of Sound have developed an awakening process of soul, a clear, faultless method of spiritual practice which brings all freedom, wisdom, and love to the sincere student. The Master and the spiritual energy of Sound can transform you from one who seeks truth into one who lives truth. Those who follow these precepts discover that this promised reward is well worth their sincere efforts, but to become one who dwells within the glory of truth, we must first find truth. This process could never be completely described; still it does have identifiable steps.

The first phase of the awakening process is the art of discrimination. Before we can come to know who or what we truly are, we must see clearly who or what we are not. With the guidance of the Master, we learn spiritual discrimination to separate our attitudes, opinions, and false identifications from our true nature as soul. This process of negation involves learning to center our attention in the third eye, and attempting to hold it there. As we live our daily lives and attempt to hold our attention within the third eye, we find that we are inundated with all kinds of thoughts, feelings, and attitudes which attempt to dominate our attention and our points of view. Every thought, action, and feeling appears to have a life of its own as the millions of points of view within the human consciousness assail us; and our mind attempts to identify with them all.

Many seekers feel the process of "dis-identification" from the mind and ego to be rather elementary and believe themselves to be above these mundane conditions. This attitude of being beyond the simple problem of identification usually is far from the true spiritual detachment the Masters teach. The mind wants to be proud of the human identity and all the various roles it fulfills. It sees nothing limiting in considering itself to be a good husband or wife, a super mom or dad, or a stellar employer or employee, and it derives great pleasure and reasons for living through these temporary, ever-changing identifications.

When we attempt to focus our attention within the third eye, we often find the passions of lust, anger, greed, vanity, and attachment very much alive and well. These passions of the mind lead our attention outward into the world. Our desires for worldly fulfillment and our fears of losing the objects of our desires rob us of our ability to control our attention. The illusions of living in a world of seeking pleasure and avoiding pain replace the spiritual reality of being soul, which exists above all the dualism of the lower dimensions of experience.

Soul exists, truth exists, and divine love exists, but not within the jungle of motives, desires, and fears which comprise the human state of consciousness. Therefore, the first step on the divine sojourn of soul is discrimination—learning to determine which thoughts, feelings, emotions, and actions are beneficial to us spiritually, and which are not. We become hunters of our selves. By continually focusing attention within the third eye, we slowly begin to see that our real self does not exist within the racing mind, the proud or fragile ego, or the many expressive modes of the personality. We gradually learn to play the role of the witness, the impartial observer, and patiently watch the incessant workings of our minds.

Through this process, the self emerges as what remains when we have discovered what we are not. Once the false has been seen as false, we no longer feel the need to give life to it. The state of calm serenity which the Masters call detachment now easily and naturally becomes our own. The rewards of the awakening process are almost immediate. Although complete awakening may take time, its dividends are paid daily. As this awakening process unfolds, the crippling tensions which occasionally grip us are greatly reduced. Fear of failure is replaced by a keen interest in new challenges, with general disregard for success or failure. Circumstances aside, life itself becomes the object of living and is its own reward. We begin to experience a new freedom from concern over economic and emotional security.

As we closely examine our attitudes and emotional reactions to life's circumstances, it becomes apparent that hardly anyone is spiritually free. We depend on everything from a good meal to a good roll in the hay to a healthy balance in our checking account for our happiness, and when we don't get these paltry chattels, we aren't happy anymore. As we become aware that not all thoughts and feelings are of equal value, we expose how many of our firmly held opinions and attitudes limit true freedom, which comes only from the viewpoint of soul. Many seekers philosophically agree with the spiritual principle that pure truth and pure love cannot be found in the outside world. They understand its rationale, and consider themselves to be in harmony with this lofty spiritual truth, but even the smallest slight from their mate, lover, or child causes them dismay. "How can he or she treat me this way? How inconsiderate, rude, and unloving can they be?" Such reactions show that particularly in their immediate areas of attachment they still are seeking truth, love, and their fulfillment in the outside worlds. Is this spiritual freedom?

We must learn the art of discrimination to see human consciousness for what it is. The awakening process does not take the route of psychology, self-help, or self-improvement. No, the Masters teach that we are already pure truth, pure love, and innately free in soul; and we really have no changes to make within the mind or the human level of consciousness. All we need to do is learn the subtle, spiritual art of centering our attention in the third eye. This method of the Masters awakens the Audible Life Stream—the source of the spiritual consciousness and home to the viewpoint of soul. Our debilitating and self-defeating attitudes and fears of the mind (the human consciousness) simply dry up as we practice discrimination and no longer feed them with all our spiritual attention.

The Fruits of Freedom

Death, for the world, is the greatest fear,
But fills my heart with bliss.

Kabir
Author, poet, weaver
15th century Master of Light and Sound

All creatures big or small are His,
And He is the Lord of all;
Whom shall I call bad
When there is none but He?

Guru Amar Das
16th century Sikh Guru

The mind loves war. Therefore, if you desire war, wage it within
your own heart. Disarm your heart of every hope and fear and vain
desire. That is the only war worth waging. Engage yourself in such
a war, and you shall no longer find the time for other wars. Peace,
serenity, and tranquility manifest only after such an encounter.

Sri Gary Olsen
1948 –
Author and Master of Light and Sound

Our many desires for fulfillment within the worlds of duality
can never fulfill our urgent spiritual desires. The Master's duty and
intention is to move us beyond our lower selves. As the awakening
process within the spiritual heart of a true student continues, the
benefits of the Master and his teachings become ever more apparent. Life in the awakened state of spiritual consciousness brings us
liberation, freedom, wisdom, and love. The Master acts to show his
students how our mental and emotional baggage has weighed
down the airy, fresh nature of spirit—the Sound Current. All truth
is approached through illusion. We come to the Master bound in
illusion, and in the end, the Master's work, coupled with our sincere
effort, always produces freedom and joy.

Although many seekers easily recognize physical and emotional
trauma as karmic events, few seekers recognize our mental and

emotional attitudes as being the cause of our karma. Most of us, if we are to make spiritual progress, come into this lifetime with two or three major karmic issues to address—conditions of the mind, attitudes such as fear, anger, boredom, or apathy that act as psychic shields or deflectors which ward off higher consciousness and prevent the true self from emerging from our being. Fear comes in many forms—some blatant, and others very subtle. The offspring of fear—procrastination, avoidance, shyness, etc.—often dress in such filmy garments that they are nearly undetectable.

We arrive at the Master's doorstep in need of assistance. Upon asking for the Master's guidance and spiritual assistance, we often discover things get a bit worse before they get better as the mental and emotional attitudes which have enslaved us must be challenged. The Masters do not dissolve our karmas into thin air, but bring us through our self-created spiritual darkness, step-by-step, as we confront our rationalizing minds which have failed to see our dilemmas. Situations which have been deeply buried often rise to the surface, and we experience some turmoil. This spiritual release sometimes shocks unwary seekers.

Those who overcome the initial shock of the Master's presence, and thus the awakening of the spiritual energy of Sound within their consciousness, find that the benefits of the Master and his teachings have already begun. Generally, it is only our faith that the Master is acting for our spiritual benefit that allows us to face our karmas at all. Then, through our experiences, we soon transcend even provisional faith, and discover knowingness. We begin to realize that the Master's words are true, his guidance is perfect, and his promises are real, as we see so many minor miracles, undeniable coincidences and events, beautifully orchestrated dreams, and real-life experiences all laid out for us. Now armed with knowingness, we are no longer shackled with old, lingering fears and doubts; we come into greater areas of responsibility for ourselves and our actions. Our human relations improve greatly, and cheerfulness and contentment become our companions.

As each of us unites with the transforming spiritual energy of Sound, soul's unerring mode of action, the spiritual quality of knowingness, replaces the old doubts of "Am I doing the right thing?" We come to know that our internal guidance and direction are faultless and ever-present. This knowingness replaces fear, doubt, and skepticism in ever-growing waves of spiritual truth and love for soul, the Sound, and the transcendental Master (our true self!) within. Fret and worry over external conditions such as security, health, money, love, and prestige are replaced by contentment. If we desire the Master's help, we need only be aware of the Divine presence at all times, and rest assured that all is being orchestrated for our higher good.

How many people are truly content, circumstances aside? Contentment is an outgrowth of the divine journey of soul and the awakening of the latent Sound. As you continue to explore, identify with, and live more within your true self, contentment emerges naturally. Contentment is never a condition of the mind, for the mind knows only relative peace, depending on external and internal conditions. The discovery of the true self brings contentment when soul rests ever-peaceful in the arms of the Divine.

Clarity of vision, the power and ability to see and understand things through spiritual objectivity, is a product of the spiritual consciousness, not a function of the mind. Clarity puts the word *know* into knowingness. Only soul's spiritual journey can bring the gift of clarity to you. Clarity shows us the true from the false; it destroys the web of illusion and transcends logic, reason, and subconscious urges. It is the ability to see false fears and desires as illusion. The mind sees only through the web of karma which includes our genetic makeup and our present-life conditioning from parents, school, and society; it can never provide true spiritual vision. When the "seeing" faculty of soul is awakened and enlivened, then clarity becomes a part of our spiritual lives.

The Masters of Sound help develop within us the ability to see things as they truly are. This aspect of soul is so well developed in true Masters that they often say that all human beings give the appearance of being asleep—or dead. This seemingly cold statement proves true as we undertake the divine journey of soul and experience clarity of vision. This clarity is not clairvoyance or astral vision. Those psychic faculties used to see thought forms and auras, even to prophesy, are very limited when compared to true spiritual vision or clarity. Clairvoyance still deals with the worlds of matter, energy, space, and time (the lower worlds of duality); true clarity lies beyond the planes of illusion.

Fear is a much greater enemy of the seeker than is desire. Our desires for love from others, respect for a job well done, and all external attachments are only our unconscious attempts to escape our fears. Even though we may feel as though we are above the many fears of the human consciousness that conditioning instills, we race feverishly from desire to desire and pleasure to pleasure, trying to escape our fears and the ensuing pain that fear delivers, always seeking shelter from the storm. Responsibility becomes a burden rather than a method of liberation, and our innate fear of dying is exceeded only by our fear of truly living. We pursue anything to escape the uneasy feelings of the small self in the large world of danger and fear.

Our desires become so well rationalized that we cannot see the real reason for their existence. Only a higher level of awareness can possibly allow the seeker to escape. Unraveling our fears and exposing desire's true nature are the Master's stock-in-trade. The Master's first duty is to free us from our fears, and his unique spiritual methods allow us to see truth from soul's viewpoint, slowing the racing mind to a tranquil, expectant stillness. As our tensions lessen and fears lose their grip, a newer, lighter spiritual vibration of truth and beauty replaces the confused, chaotic ramblings of the unenlightened mind; and serenity and true seeing become our reality.

Perhaps no greater gift exists than the promise that our personal will can be transmuted into divine will. All the trials and tribulations of life can be traced back to the inherent conflict between these two opposing forces, both of which exist within each of us. The personal will, the self-directed mode of living, exists only in the human consciousness. It brings acquisition or poverty, conditional love or the lack of it, and knowledge or ignorance. As seekers, we have chosen to locate and actuate the divine will within ourselves; this separates us from ordinary people, even the religious ones.

Divine will cannot be found within the playground of the human consciousness. It exists for us only when we yearn deeply for human consciousness to be transcended and the spiritual consciousness to be born. Divine will within propels us to self-realization—first to discover soul and then to come to realize it as our true identity. When this goal of the journey of soul is reached, divine will leads us onward to God realization—to our realization of the God within. Now the divine will gains full expression and releases its unique intention through the vehicle of soul. The goals and intentions of the Master and his teachings are no less than this for each of us.

The Masters of Sound promise self-realization and God realization to each of us. Soul is sleeping in its cradle within the body, lulled to sleep by the gentle lullaby of illusion. The Master exists to provide the vital connection between our slumbering soul and the divine Sound Current within.

CHAPTER 10

NO GREATER LOVE EXISTS

God is love and we have got love innate in our own selves. It must have something to love. Whom should we love? Guru Nanak said, "Peace be unto all the world over, under Thy will, O God." God resides in every heart and our souls are of the same essence as that of God. So if we love God, naturally we will love everybody.

Kirpal Singh
1894 – 1974
Author, lecturer, former president of the
United Nations World Fellowship of Religions

Banish duality from your heart,
    and be free from all disputes;
The Turk and the Hindu are not different.
Look on all as holy, not as thieves,
    for the Lord is in every single one.

Bulleh Shah
18th century Muslim saint
Disciple of Shah Inayat

No greater love exists than the love of the Divine for Its children. The cardinal principle of all the worlds is that soul exists because the Creator loves it. So great is Its love for each of us that God has graced each and every soul with a part of Itself.

Soul has been given eternal life and the awesome, divine power of creation. We have been given our own ship and have been appointed captain. We have been given our own world with the authority to be king, bureaucrat, or peasant. Few understand the nature of our divine inheritance, and fewer still take responsibility for the guardianship of our divine trust.

Just as a robin shoves its fledglings from the nest, and parents send their children out into the world, the Creator pushed soul into the worlds of duality so that it may come to know itself. Can the young robin discover its own nature if it remains forever in the nest, under its mother's protective wing? Can our children ever discover themselves if we keep them home, sheltered from the world? Before the young robin is sent out to fly, it is nourished, cared for, and loved by its parents. Before we send our children into the world, we make great effort to prepare them. Similarly, before the Creator sent soul for its sojourn in the worlds of duality, It prepared soul with the road map back home, and endowed it with Its own divine qualities and attributes.

The robin is first cause in her own nest; and we as parents are first cause in our own homes, just as soul is first cause within its own world, and the Supreme One is first cause in all the worlds. The divine chain of responsibility has made soul, armed with all the god-like qualities, the general in its own theater of operations. The Creator has placed Its trust in soul to act in its own behalf—and therefore, in the Creator's behalf—wherever, whenever, and however it acts. But as we look into the worlds of duality, it is apparent that a coup has occurred. Soul's power of creation and ability to control our attention and our attitudes has been usurped by the ego and the personality. It is as if the young robin has left the nest and decided that it was in fact an ant and refused to fly!

In the physical worlds, no greater love exists than the love of the Master for each and every one who calls for help. The Master's spiritual mission is to assist all souls to become their own masters; to escape the slavery of the ego, mind, personality, and emotions; and to regain control of their five-bodied constitutions (physical, astral, causal, mental, soul). Due to the overwhelming power of the negative forces within the physical worlds, the depths and complexity of our illusions are simply too great for us to overcome unaided. However, the bond of love that exists between all sincere students and a true Master is strong enough to overcome all obstacles on the path to spiritual liberation. When this mission is complete, we no longer exist as students; rather we become a living center of spiritual vibration, attuned to the Divine within.

As children of God, we are destined to become strong, spiritually powerful, free, and wise. Born to be kings, we will never be content until we deservedly assume the throne. Our birthright and spiritual heritage demand that we, as seekers and heirs to the spiritual kingdom within, learn the land and the laws of our kingdom. The Master and his teachings are here for us so that we may come to ascend our thrones and rule lovingly and wisely. Soul can display no greater love than to take command of its own destiny and return the love with which it has been blessed to its Creator. No greater love exists.

Where Are You Headed?

An ounce of practice is better than a ton of knowledge. What use is it to know the principles if one does not live them? It is infinitely better to practice than to preach.

Maharaj Sardar Bahadur Jagat Singh
Author, lecturer
20th century Master of Light and Sound

Blessed is the person who always keeps his eye on the goal.

Rumi
Poet, Muslim saint of Persia
13th century Master of Light and Sound

Most individuals and even many seekers give a geographic response to the question "Where are you from?" Others may name their parents and recite their ancestry. A few may be aware of past incarnations and excitedly relate their previous experiences within the physical or astral worlds. Although most sincere spiritual seekers feel that they are soul and children of the Divine, generally they allow illusion and delusion to prevail, and they have little, if any, true recognition of their divine origin.

The purpose of the journey of soul is to awaken us to our true identity and allow soul to recapture the glorious nature of its birthright. In making this quest for liberation our foundation, we must be equipped with a sincere desire to know truth and a willingness to follow our hearts in its pursuit. Without this spiritual armor, our search will involve only mere speculation, philosophizing, and seeking the idea of truth rather than experiencing its reality.

Those true spiritual seekers whose sincerity and willingness are pure are always led to the level of truth they need to experience and actuate at that time. The unerring nature of the Creator leads them to the path that will best fulfill their innate desire to more fully experience the Divine within. True seekers realize that divine guidance is infallible, beyond question or reproach. But while the seeker knows where he or she wants to go, will the mind go where only the heart can lead? This is when we encounter the issue of trust. Many claim to be willing and loudly profess their sincerity to their friends, the Master, or anyone who will listen. But can they really claim to be sincere and willing without the ability to trust their own hearts? Those who trust in the Creator trust in their own hearts.

Only the brave, the bold, and the courageous go forward on the spiritual path to freedom. We eagerly anticipate freedom; we long to be enraptured by divine love; we envision a life lived in wisdom —but do we acknowledge the magnitude of the illusion in which we currently live? Do we understand how we ourselves created this deception? Are we willing to examine our own level of ignorance and delusion? Many want the Creator, but few know where they come from and where they are going.

All life has come from the Creator and all life is headed home— to the Creator. We each have a date with destiny, and the Creator is that destiny. Time is not really an issue; we may take all the time we need and do what we want to do. But after we have experienced millions of lifetimes in bondage to the world, and the mind has become weary, we are restless. Divine discontent manifests, and we are no longer nourished or satisfied through the ordinary means to happiness. The darkest hour is indeed the one which precedes the dawn, and within this hour, it is always wise to remember that just as the past created the present, the present creates the future.

The action or reaction we choose within any moment of time is the springboard which propels us into the next moment. How many times have we felt that we were in harmony with soul, that we had the bull (the mind and ego) by the horns, and suddenly the next moment we were gored mercilessly and left wondering, "How did this happen when everything was going so well? How did we so completely lose our grip?" Two traits essential to all truth seekers must be an awareness of our current attitudes, which define us through our identification with them, and the desire to escape our self-created prison. In returning to our Creator, the one quality we must avoid is rigidity of attitude or point of view.

The Masters of Sound state that we must want liberation very much and for a very long time before it is won. Our failures, our loss of perspective, and our lack of control of the divine faculty of attention are integral parts in the life of all seekers. All success and failure must be balanced in the eyes of the Lord. A sense of humor and the tingling feeling which arises from bathing in the warm waters of contentment should be our companions on the journey of soul. The quality which will bring us through the worst of times is perseverance, coupled with a deep sense of willingness to always walk the path. Fortunately, we will never be alone.

Soul's journey to unite with its Creator is simultaneously the most profound, startling experience of life, and the most subtle, invisible, timeless sojourn imaginable. It comes and goes like a ghost in the night, and yet it is ever present.

Before soul can be reunited with the One, it must come to understand the many, so soul's voyage home is an experience in consciousness. We travel from human awareness to the Kingdom of God through many, many states of consciousness, much like getting in a car in California and driving to Virginia. We pass through diverse lands; but more importantly, we encounter a multiplicity of differing attitudes, points of view, and many states of consciousness along the way—all karmic conditions, passions of the mind (lust, anger, greed, vanity, attachment), and emotional feelings toward life. These points of view, when separated from soul, are no longer the One, but the many. It is the nature of the lower bodies (physical, astral, causal, mental) to divide and separate these attitudes from the Divine Essence and make them real through identifying with them. For example, anger or lust always exists within us, as do love and tranquility. They are part of the whole of pure consciousness, which is God's creation. If something disturbs us or doesn't meet our expectations, and if we choose to identify with anger, we become angry. We have separated anger from pure consciousness and entered into the state of consciousness called anger.

A journey from California to Virginia can be long or short, depending on how many stops we choose to make. Identifying with any particular state of consciousness is a roadblock or a detour at best, and if we are not careful, becomes a destination. This does not mean we never get angry or experience emotional joy. There is nothing wrong with experiencing joy or anger, if we recognize we have chosen to do so. Usually when we become aware that we create our lives through our attitudes, we begin choosing and controlling them more carefully. We must recognize the form and existence of the parts before we see the whole.

As soul gains more and more control within the many states of consciousness it can manifest, life becomes more real, meaningful, and enjoyable. The rat race, deceit, and the endless sense of yearning which characterize the human state of consciousness fade in memory and are replaced by the joy and contentment of life within the moment of time. Soul's will becomes one with divine will. When one enters into partnership with the Divine, discontent and disappointment disappear. The raging river that was once our consciousness flattens out into a broad, placid stream. Rather than being slaves to circumstances and karma, we become the makers and masters of the moment as soul's love, wisdom, and power are channeled into the miraculous unfoldment of the Creator's grand plan; and soul becomes a co-worker with the Divine. There is no greater joy or sense of accomplishment than that of being in harmony with soul and its spiritual desires. This is where we are headed; this is the road which not only leads to home, but is home. All heaven and all good is right here, right now.

The question of the moment is so simple that any child can penetrate it. It all boils down to "What do you want?" We all know that people generally do what they want to do. This is the prime motivator of all time and all action. Without true commitment, spiritual truth will not be enlivened. Again, we must want truth very much, and for a very long time before the moment becomes our own. Finding and actuating love, wisdom, power, beauty, and truth with only our minds and wills as our resources is like making the journey from California to Virginia on our hands and knees with no food or water. The journey of soul is more than a rocky road; it is paved with illusion, the map is a labyrinth, and the guardrails are all painted black.

The seeker is not free. We cannot choose to follow the Master. Life, the Divine One, and the Master within (our own true self) choose us. When the student is ready, the Master appears. This age-old maxim cannot be overlooked. Only our false notions lead us to believe that we can pick and choose the Master, as we would an apple at the market. The Creator's design is far too intricate and exact to allow for that. It is the seeker whose karma determines his or her circumstances in life. It is also the seeker who is headed home. The Master has already arrived. The Master is free. He holds the key, which fits all the locks that bind us. The locks have different sizes and shapes; some are iron; and some, gold; but His key fits them all.

AFTERWORD

Our loving Creator has placed the path back to Itself within our own being. Once our desire to experience truth and the love of God becomes a sincere petition, moving us to still our minds and open our hearts to inner promptings, our petition is always answered. All spiritual endeavors are entered into less by choice than by readiness. It is certainly a great truism that when a seeker is ready for the reality of a deeper spiritual experience, then somehow, in some unique way, one is afforded an opportunity to grow into that experience.

It has been my great fortune to have been a student of Light and Sound for 23 years. My Sat Guru bestowed his highest initiation, that of God realization, on me on November 8, 1994. I only had to go inside to meet the God that lives within us all.

Your spiritual journey is your own affair, and its direction is a product of your receptivity to the divine guidance ever present within. My purpose in writing this book is only to provide you with the gift of knowledge or further knowledge of the teachings of Light and Sound, and to offer my conclusions for your further investigation, should you be so moved.

Respectfully,

Dennis R. Holtje
Santa Fe, New Mexico
July 1995

If you should desire further information regarding the teachings of Light and Sound, please write to:
MasterPath, Inc. (non-profit)
P.O. Box 9035
Temecula, CA 92589-9035

The Requirements For Walking a True Sound Path

Maintaining a spiritual and mental balance while simultaneously fulfilling obligations to family and society, are extremely important. If the gates of heaven are rushed indiscriminately in an effort to forego earthly responsibilities, failure results. We do not attempt to escape the world, but rather seek to learn the values it teaches.

Some individuals experience extreme difficulty in managing the affairs of daily life due to conditions of mental or emotional instability such as major depression, bi-polar disorders, schizophrenia, or multiple personality disorders (and their treatments). <u>An attempt to open the spiritual centers while these disorders exist should not be undertaken.</u> The student must have a stable mind in order to embark on a path of sound. A seeker who has these conditions would be more purely served by focusing on acquiring greater mental stability in negotiating one's daily life, as this is a necessary foundation for any pursuit of the higher worlds of consciousness.

A *Sound* Path embraces all virtues of extant religions and beyond. Obstacles are purposefully present initially to counter one's spiritual ascent, yet the true seeker desiring God allows other needs and desires to become secondary, while soul attempts to connect with the Audible Life Stream.

No one enters the Path in a state of purity, and thus some feel trepidacious and somewhat self-conscious as to their readiness for the spiritual ascent. *A pure, heartfelt search for truth is simple yet imperative.* Once the Sound Current is sufficiently flowing through one's beingness, lesser obstacles fall away naturally by their own weight, for now the mind has something it loves more dearly. The mind only releases the old when something greater takes its place. The Sound Current shows its utter majesty and purity of purpose in being the *greater*.

The means of accomplishment that humankind has been given to achieve the higher consciousness manifests when the devotee ascends to a truer level of sincerity. All yearn for the higher life in God, feel the inner tugs and pulls, but only after a certain stage is truth laid bare. The woes and miseries of life become unbearable, compounded by an intense feeling of separation from the Lord. The sensitive individuals internally safeguard their true feelings, allowing their involvement in life to become robotic, conditional, mundane.

If one has the will to liberation strongly implanted in consciousness, and is willing to face whatever comes with purity of purpose and personal responsibility, nothing will hold one back.

A seeker who experiences and responds to an inner call to awaken often delves into various psychic practices such as healing, past-life regressions, aura adjusting, trance channeling, astral projection, astrology, religion, psychology, and philosophy, in attempts to discover truth using the mental, emotional, or physical senses. Sincere investigation of the *light* and *sound* necessitates a willingness and spiritual readiness to acknowledge the limitations of such practices in order to release them in provisional faith that the Sound Current within may lead to the cherished goal. *Continued involvement with practices which enliven the mental, emotional, and physical senses, while attempting to awaken soul and the Sound Current within, can prove dangerous and misleading.* When a seeker continues such practices, the psychic worlds create a stronger draw than the *light* and *sound*, and one should rightfully fulfill this avenue until the draw diminishes, readying the student for proper entry into the *sound*.

GLOSSARY

ADI GRANTH – 17th century compilation of the writings of Light and Sound gurus of the 15th and 16th centuries. Compiled by the 5th Sikh Guru, Arjan Dev.

ANGER – One of the five negative passions of the mind.

ASCENDED MASTER – Any true Master or Saint who is no longer active in the physical worlds and who has ascended to the higher spiritual regions.

ASTRAL BODY – The radiant body. A finer and lighter body than the physical body; the instrument of expression used in the astral region. Soul's vehicle for experiencing human love, anger, fear, desire, etc.

ASTRAL PLANE – The exoteric name of the first spiritual region.

ASTRAL PROJECTION – A phenomenon in which the inner bodies split from the physical body to travel only as far as the astral world, encumbered by all emotional, mental, and karmic baggage.

ASTROLOGY – The study of the Zodiac; uses mechanical principles such as charts, etc., to predict the future; can only state the possibility of events that might occur; the study of the human personality; the study of births and deaths in the lower worlds. Relies on the light to reveal apparent reality.

ATTACHMENT – A state of bondage of the lower bodies (physical, astral, causal, mental) to karmic patterns of life that keep one in the physical consciousness which creates enslavement to the physical realm and desires, connections, identification with objects, family, belongings, etc.

ATTRIBUTE – A characteristic or quality. Creation of the world was made possible by the interplay of three attributes or qualities that exist in the human body: harmony; action or activity; and inertia or darkness. All life continually vacillates within these three.

AUDIBLE LIFE STREAM – God expressing Itself in a stream which is both visible and audible (Light and Sound); the sustaining life force; also known as the Sound Current flowing out from the Supreme Creative center of the Universe of universes; life force that can be heard and seen with the spiritual vision and hearing faculties of soul; the all-embracing spiritual force which composes life and makes up all elemental substances including the component parts of soul.

AURA – A luminous radiation of fine vibratory waves or rays of color surrounding the physical frame which originate in thoughts and emotions.

AWAKENED SOUL – Soul, awake and functioning, while still living in the physical state in its physical body.

B

BEING – The choosing of an identity. That which is, as distinguished from that which is not; a part of the trinity of soul (knowing, being, seeing); the conscious choosing and implementing of one's true spiritual identity. Action apart from the *control* of mind, ego, emotions, and personality; being incorporates all but is not limited by any faculty or perception.

BEINGNESS – Soul; the manifested individual beingness of spirit, created with the power to create, form postulates, form opinions, imagine, and have intelligence.

BRAHM – The power that creates and dissolves. The negative power in the lower worlds. Believed by many to be a god, but actually a minor subordinate of the Divine. Lord of the OM portion of the Audible Life Stream.

C

CAUSAL BODY – Also called "seed body," because the seeds of all karmas reside in it; all actions or karmas manifest in the lower bodies (physical, emotional, mental).

CAUSAL PLANE – The plane of consciousness within all souls which stores karmic records and accounts; the seed body. The location of the time track—past, present, future.

CHAKRAS – Major energy centers in the human body; each looks like a small wheel, with parts that suggest the petals of a lotus. The primary chakras are the rectal, reproductive, naval, heart, throat, third eye, and crown centers.

CLAIRVOYANCE – The awareness of seeing and knowing in the psychic worlds.

CONSCIOUSNESS – Attention; the state of awareness in which an individual lives daily. Can be divided into two parts: the outer consciousness in which a sense of reality is created by dependence on the physical senses and the sense organs; or the inner consciousness which creates true reality through contact with the Audible Life Stream. *(See also: Four states of Consciousness.)*

CONTEMPLATION – A spiritual exercise during which attention is centered on a definite spiritual principle, thought, or idea, or upon the Master. An action which gives purpose to the focusing of attention, differing from the more passive experience of meditation. An active spiritual experience in which the practitioner centers attention upon a situation in order to see truth; seeing the whole which includes all parts; giving purpose to the focusing of attention; unrestrained examination of any spiritual idea; the 360-degree viewpoint.

COSMIC CONSCIOUSNESS – Spiritual insight given to the intellectual senses in the mental realm; the first step in consciousness toward reaching soul, before self-realization.

CREATIVE POWER – Spirit, identical with life, love, beauty, and wisdom that comes from the Divine Source, manifested by thought; possible because of the consciousness of oneness of the individual with Spirit, by both the individual and Spirit.

CREATOR – The prime mover of the Universal Body (whereas soul is the prime mover in its own universe); creative action that manifests out of awareness of being the image and likeness of God. That which all opposites have in common; the Audible Life Stream issues forth from It.

D

DESIRE – The thirst for material worldly objects. Desire originates within the senses; love of and for objects. The desires of the senses control the mind and entrap the soul.

DETACHMENT – A state of being in which reaction to the world and the physical, emotional, and mental senses are replaced by the viewpoint of soul. Particularly, a mental detachment from the world and worldly desires; a state of mind—not to be confused with asceticism, renunciation of the world, or non-action.

DISCIPLINE – Active state of monitoring and controlling viewpoint or attention; involvement in self-surrender and self-control; true discipline is the subjective control of emotions and imagination.

DISCRIMINATION – Spiritually separating the real from the apparent, the changing from the changeless, and the true from the false, through inquiry, study, and centering within the third eye.

DIVINE – The One and unchanging Being; not to be confused with the powers or personifications located at each chakra and plane.

DIVINE FACULTY – The imagination; the inner action, desire, picturing, expecting, creating.

DIVINE LAW – All things continually exist as a manifestation from and by the Sound Current power. Soul is the greatest achievement of creation, exists throughout eternity, loves and seeks its Creator and will attain the highest glory.

DIVINE SPIRIT – The Sound; the Voice; that Essence, the Holy Ghost, the Comforter that gives life to all; the Sound Current, the Audible Life Stream.

DIVINE TRUTH – The One and unchanging Spirit; separation or a divided state of The Creator is illusion; the Oneness of The Creator.

DIVINE WILL – Absolute Will; the will or desire of God; the principles of God, which when followed, lead to spiritual unfoldment.

DOCTRINE – In spiritual definition, the universal principles; that which is true and divinely created; universal law.

DOGMA – Man-made laws and teachings; morals; taboos. Concrete beliefs based on custom and tradition; deals with the duality of right and wrong rather than the middle road.

DUAL WORLDS – The worlds of matter, energy, space, and time; of negative and positive; of male and female. All the worlds below the soul plane: physical, astral, causal, mental, and etheric planes.

DYING DAILY – Separating the attention from the body consciousness at will for soul transport; coming and going at will between the physical and higher worlds through the soul power; dying while still living; also implies the daily purification process.

E

EGO – Psychic consciousness within the body.

ENERGY – The life-force of soul, apart from the lower manifestations which empower the lower planes (physical, astral, causal, mental).

ESOTERIC – Secret knowledge or hidden meaning. *(See also: exoteric.)*

ESSENCE OF SPIRIT – Nobility, aesthetics, life, love, and beauty, and the single primary impulse to express truth; the love and beauty it feels Itself to be; the breath of God.

ETHICS – That which is selfless, is good for the whole; will not harm one and will do justice for all concerned. Actions for the benefit of all.

EXOTERIC – Teachings which are visible and audible to the human eye and ear. *(See also: esoteric.)*

EXTRA-SENSORY PERCEPTION – Moving mind and thoughts beyond self and the recognition of events between self and others, or outside the self-environment.

F

FAITH – The initial stage of spiritual inquiry; confidence in a belief. The building block of all religions.

FATE KARMA – One's destiny in life, created by actions in past lives, and upon which present life is based. The third eye opens when the majority of fate karma is resolved. *(See also: Karma.)*

FEAR – An emotion originating in the astral consciousness. Can become a state of mind which immobilizes and distorts consciousness through anger, worry, sentimental emotionalism, and envy; a way of preventing spiritual unfoldment. *(See also: Hatred.)*

FIRST CAUSE – The act of creation; soul's conscious will overriding karmic tendencies. God, Master, spirit, and soul are first cause; mind, emotion, and karma are second cause, or effect.

FIVE FACES OF THE MASTER – Outer Master; Dream Master; Radiant Form of the Master; Spiritual Form of the Master; and the True Master (Sat Guru).

FIVE MELODIES – The Sound Current's audible manifestation on the major planes of experience (physical, astral, causal, mental, soul).

FIVE PASSIONS OF THE MIND – The forces through which the negative force controls and keeps soul in the lower worlds: lust, anger, greed, attachment, and vanity.

FIVE VIRTUES – The antidotes to the passions of the mind: discrimination, forgiveness, contentment, detachment, and humility.

FOUR STATES OF CONSCIOUSNESS – The four states with which soul works in following the spiritual path: Sleep, Dream, Awake, and Super-consciousness.

FREE WILL – Each soul has the right and power to decide to follow either the lower or higher forces; our individual spiritual right, which is usually a burden until self-realization is attained.

G

GIFT WAVES – The Master's gifts to soul in consciousness; movements in consciousness marked by love flow and clear perception.

GOD CONSCIOUSNESS – The state of realization experienced just prior to God realization.

GOD REALIZATION – Soul matured; awareness and mastery of truth; union with the Divine Essence; the true Master's abode; the ultimate goal of any seeker; the purpose of all life. Realization of the God state; the knowledge of God; attainment of the higher spiritual state of the supernatural life; uniting the human and the divine natures.

GOD REALIZED – A supreme saint; a saint who has attained God realization.

GOD SEEKERS – Those who search for the realization of God, not knowing that it is always with them.

GURU – Literally, one who gives light; a spiritual teacher; master; preceptor; guide. *(See also: Sat Guru.)*

H

HARMONY – The perception that the "I AM" is ONE, always in harmony with Itself, including all things because there is no second creative power; complete acceptance and oneness.

HATRED – One of the two negative emotions that comes out of the stream of thought consciousness; the other emotion is fear.

HEALING – Spiritual unfoldment due to the action of the Master and the student; replacing the lower levels of consciousness with the higher levels; whereas a "healer" replaces one state of consciousness with another state within the same level of consciousness.

HOLY SPIRIT – The offshoot of the Sound Current which sustains all life in the lower worlds (physical, astral, causal, mental). (The Holy Spirit of the Christian doctrine is the universal mind power, originating on the mental plane.)

HUMAN CONSCIOUSNESS – The lower or earth state of understanding; the state of consciousness facilitated by the lower forces as its channel.

I

IGNORANCE – Unawareness; source of bondage in the lower worlds.

IMAGINATION – A mental faculty that God has given soul so that it may enter into the first door of the inner worlds; a function which allows soul to image in thought.

IMMORTALITY – The state of being changeless and deathless, opposite of mortality or being subject to change and death.

IMPATIENCE – Within the passion of anger, the quality or tendency of mind to expect results without regard for divine timing.

INITIATION – The true spiritual sacrament; the connection between soul and the Audible Life Stream. A true Sat Guru can initiate and awaken any soul into the Sound Current.

INNER HEARING – The hearing faculty of soul. *(See also: Surat.)*

INNER MASTER – The eternal Master; synonymous with the Sound Current Master; direct personification of the Audible Life Stream; the true Master, imperishable, and eternally present in the now.

INNER TEACHINGS – The teachings which go beyond the intellectual senses and enter into the depth of wisdom; the most sublime, sacred, secret wisdom of all things, given by the Inner Master, mostly in the inner world.

INNER VISION – That attention of seeing which does not use the physical eyes, but "sees" with the inner eyes. *(See also: Nirat.)*

INTELLECT – The capacity of the mind to study various laws originating from the different relations of things to one another; not life in itself but a function of life; an effect and not the cause; does not create anything entirely new or constructive.

INTUITION – A faculty of acquiring knowing without using the senses, without reasoning; an innate, instinctive awareness.

K

KARMA – Action; the law of cause and effect; action and reaction; the debits and credits resulting from our deeds, which bring us back to the worlds in future lives to reap their fruits. There are four types of karma:

Original karma – karma of the beginning; not earned by the individual, but established by The Creator in the beginning.

Fate karma – past actions that are responsible for our present conditions; that portion of our karma which is allotted to this life and is responsible for our present existence.

Present karma – the result of actions during the present life.

Stored karma – the balance of unpaid karmas from all our past lives; the store of karma located in the causal plane to be worked off or to bear fruit in future incarnations.

KARMIC IMPRESSIONS – Impressions or tendencies from previous lives, early upbringing, traditions, and social influences, which shape the basic outlook and behavior patterns of a human being. Can be positive, negative, or spiritual.

KARMIC PATTERNS – The habitual ways in which an individual acts and reacts throughout the experiences of many lives.

KEY TO SPIRITUAL WORLDS – The detached state from both worldly desires and a mental love of the world; state of complete detachment from all duality; non-attachment in which one does not reject material things, but lives in a state of not being controlled by them.

KINGDOM OF GOD – The consciousness of God within soul.

KINGDOM OF HEAVEN – The true home of soul; that realm of Spirit where God and the Sound Current have established the fountainhead in the universe of universes.

KNOWING – The ability of soul to perceive directly; above reason, logic, and all mental sensation; certainty; clarity.

L

LAW OF ATTITUDES – The law of the states of consciousness; the power of imagination that rules over will in the actions in this world: that which you imagine, you become.

LAW OF BALANCE – The equilibrium which lies in the Godhead; all is completely in balance in the Creator's universal body; the principle of unity, of oneness, but in the lower regions this unity takes on the appearance of duality or chaos.

LAW OF FACSIMILES – All effects in life are created in the mind of the individual through thoughts and images which have been gathered and stored in past and present incarnations.

LAW OF GOD – Everything has its cause in spirit; Divine Truth is one and eternal.

LAW OF LOVE – The principle which gives thought the dynamic power to connect with its object and enables it to master every unfavorable human experience; feeling that gives vitality to thought; feeling is desire and desire is love.

LAW OF POLARITY – Each thing within the universe is supported, given life, maintained by, and resistant to its opposite.

LAW OF SPIRIT – Spirit in itself is the assumption of increase; future conditions manifest out of present conditions; there is always something more to experience.

LAW OF SPIRITUAL GROWTH – Truth has to be continually rediscovered, perfected, and transmuted; the same truth has to be experienced in ever-new forms.

LAW OF VIBRATIONS – All creation in the lower worlds is carried out and manifested through harmonic vibrations. Rules all effects such as wave lengths, outflows, inflows, cause and effect, and the harmonics of the movement of Sound.

LIGHT – That which reveals the contents of the mind through reason, logic, study, and the use of the psychic senses; information, knowledge; cannot alone deliver the soul to self-realization.

LIVING MASTER – The Word made flesh, the true and capable Master who works for the liberation of entrapped souls, guiding them beyond and out of the lesser reality of existence into self-realization and eventually to Godhood.

LIVING TRUTH – Every atom is immortal and eternal; each is soul.

LOGOS – The Greek name for Word of God. Ever outward-flowing Power of God in dynamic action; created and sustains the world.

LOVE – The most powerful force in the inner worlds. The force which binds the lower worlds together through the attraction of opposite polarities, whether atomic, elemental, animal, or human. In the higher worlds it is pure essence, Light and Sound, unconditional. It is the essence of seeking balance in the union of the masculine and feminine expressions of the Divine Self.

LOWER PLANES – The physical, astral, causal, mental, and etheric planes; the regions which are the training ground for soul.

M

MACROCOSM – The world of the Creator, including all universes; the universal world, reflected in the microcosm—man. The macrocosm dwells within the body of each individual.

MASTER – A liberated soul that has attained the soul plane of consciousness; a true Saint; one who is God realized.

MATREYIA – Return of the Buddha.

MATRIX – Stating what you intend to do; an inner image.

MAYA – Illusion or delusion; deception; unreality; the phenomenal universe. That which is not eternal is not real and true. The veil of maya or illusion conceals the vision of God from one's sight.

MENTAL PLANE – State of consciousness that deals with thought, reason, logic, and intellect.

MEST – Matter, Energy, Space, and Time. The finished creation; the lower worlds.

MICROCOSM – The miniature universe; the reflection of the macrocosm.

MIDDLE PATH – The neutral way; neither black nor white, neither positive nor negative, neither masculine (forcing), nor feminine (receptive); spiritual balance between the negative and the positive; neither for nor against.

MIND – Serves as an instrument for Spirit to make all its contact with the material worlds; the channel through which the negative force controls and keeps soul in the lower worlds, through the five passions of the mind. There is only one mind acting in different bodies: the lower world mind manifesting in the common affairs of the world; the mind of the emotions; and the inner mind.

MINERAL STATE – Consciousness that is largely dormant, encased in rock-like substance of minerals. Soul experiences the physical realm through expansion, contraction, extrusion, and bonding with other elements.

N

NARROW WAY – Name given to the opening or small door located at the third eye, where Spirit enters and leaves the body and spiritual awareness occurs.

NIRAT – The seeing faculty of the soul which recognizes truth; an ability to instantaneously distinguish between spiritual consciousness (knowing, being, and seeing), and psychic or human consciousness; the attention inside; awakening of the "inner mind." *(See also: Surat.)*

NOTHINGNESS – The container of all unmanifested potential; the storehouse of knowing, being, and seeing.

NOW-NESS – The present moment; being present in the moment of time; the eternal point of life; Beingness of Truth; a stillness of all activity.

O

ORIGINAL KARMA – Karma of the beginning; not earned by the individual, but established by the Creator. *(See also: Karma.)*

OUTER MASTER – The living Master; the Word (Sound) made flesh; the true and capable Master who works for the liberation of entrapped souls, guiding them beyond and out of the lesser reality of existence into self-realization and eventually God realization.

P

PASSIONS OF THE MIND – The five passions of the mind are lust, anger, greed, attachment, and vanity (ego or pride). *(See also: Virtues for the antidotes to these passions.)*

PAST KARMA – The store of unpaid karmas from one's past lives. *(See also: Karma.)*

PATH OF SOUL – To contemplate the life, love, and beauty of Divine Power and to realize Itself as already giving expression to It as a channel in thought, feeling, and action; It is neither positive nor negative, but is the projection of consciousness through soul.

PATIENCE – Persisting with calmness and self-control with the mind firmly fixed on God, and with attention to the goal of God consciousness. The greatest discipline in all the works of Sound.

PLANES – The states of consciousness soul travels through on its way back home. An infinite number of planes blend and shift from one state of consciousness to another.

POSITIVE AND NEGATIVE – The positive is the outgoing force; the negative is the receptive force; the positive is forever changing into the negative and the negative is always in the process of becoming the positive; without one the other could not exist.

POWER – The moving force of entrapment or liberation; supreme liberation or detachment from all distractions of the lower worlds.

PRESENT KARMA – The debits and credits created by our actions in this life, to be reaped in the future. *(See also: Karma.)*

PSYCHIC – The physical, astral, causal, and mental levels of consciousness and their corresponding planes; all elements of the light including astrology, ESP, tarot, meditation, prophecy, astral projection, I Ching, psychic readings, religion, ritual, drumming, visions, etc.

PURIFICATION – Removing the fixed desires of the human nature and experiencing the power of the Sound Current; dying daily.

R

RADIANT BODY – The Light Body of the Sound Current Master.

REINCARNATION – The rebirth of soul into a new body each time it reenters this world or another. The physical body experiences death; soul is eternal.

S

SAINT – A pious or holy person; esoterically, one who has reached the fifth spiritual region or plane.

SAT GURU – In spiritual terms, a true Master, appointed before birth; one who is capable of replacing darkness with Light and Sound; he who anoints the seeker with the Sound Current. A saint who is also a spiritual teacher. Everyone who has reached the fifth spiritual region is a saint, but not all of them accept followers or are designated to teach.

SEEING – Attribute of soul which recognizes truth; ability to instantaneously distinguish between spiritual consciousness (knowing, being, and seeing), and psychic or human consciousness.

SEEKER(S) OF TRUTH – Those who search for the essence, spirit, soul and life of everything that exists or appears to exist, itself unchangeable and immortal; those who sincerely work to attain truth at any sacrifice.

SELF-DISCIPLINE – Control of the psychic self; control of the emotions and the imagination, which is subjective. Self-discipline does not imply denial.

SELF-REALIZATION – Soul recognizing its true nature and purpose; soul entering into incipient spiritual consciousness, and finding itself; the beginning of spiritual awareness. Soul entering into the first region of pure spirit, and there recognizing itself, stripped of all materialism and no longer encumbered with the lower bodies.

SOUL – Spirit; also the supreme spirit or "over-soul" of all bodies within one's personal universe. Humans' true identity; the immortal, deathless, and forever unchanging aspect of our constitution. Soul gives life to the physical, astral, mental, causal, and etheric bodies; identical with the Sound Current; a drop from the Ocean of Love and Mercy. The soul body experiences self-realization and is the only vehicle of humankind that can rise above the worlds of duality. The central core of the universes of The Creator; the true identity of all life (mineral, plant, animal, human, or psychic entity); the primary unit of consciousness or awareness; the essence of God and Its true gift of life; the deathless self which when unencumbered can experience the divine attributes.

SOUL TRANSPORT – The means by which soul is freed from the constraints and limitations of the lower bodies. Consciously assuming the viewpoint of soul; surrendering to one's innate, natural, spiritual viewpoint. Upward movement in consciousness through direct projection; transcends the grip of matter, energy, space, and time. Used to travel in and upward through the many planes of consciousness.

SOUND – The wave of consciousness or awareness which is constantly creating; the life-source; the Audible Life Stream; the transformative essence of God which draws us from the human and psychic states into the spiritual consciousness.

SOUND CURRENT – The creative power which manifests as Sound and Light in the spiritual regions. As the soul manifests in the body as consciousness, the Word of God manifests Itself as inner Spiritual Sound. The Sound Current is both *expressible*, which can be uttered, and *inexpressible*, which can only be heard within. The expressible points and leads to the real or inexpressible within—a creative power that emanates without ceasing from the Supreme Being, and takes us to It. The Audible Life Stream or breath of God; the creative power which manifests as Light and Sound; the truly transformative divine elixir.

SOUND CURRENT MASTER – The Inner Master; the changeless aspect of God which assumes any form necessary to stay in contact with all parts of Its Universal Body; can be with one or a million students at the same time; the Inner Teacher that manifests in the seeker's third eye on the astral plane.

SPIRITUAL FREEDOM – Salvation or spiritual liberation during this lifetime. True liberation is soul free from the tyranny of the physical, astral, mental, and causal bodies; and attaining union with its true source.

SPIRITUALITY – The essence of truth which is caught, not taught.

STORED KARMA – The balance of unpaid karmas from all our past lives; the store of karma located in the causal plane to be worked off or to bear fruit in future incarnations.

SUBCONSCIOUS MIND – Unconscious attitudes and habits; patterns of negative reactions that are unknown; uncontrolled mind; that which imprisons soul.

SUFI – An adherent of Sufism, a Muslim mystic sect originally from Persia.

SURAT – The hearing faculty of the soul. When soul goes within, it hears the melody of the Sound Current through "surat" and sees the light of the Sound Current through "nirat." At a certain stage the two faculties merge into one. *(See also: Nirat.)*

T

THIRD EYE – A point in the astral body, between and behind the two eyes; the eye that brings oneness to duality.

TRUE MASTER – True or perfect Master who can initiate seekers into the Sound Current; a Master who has access to the soul plane.

TRUTH – True, real, everlasting, actual, right, fit, essence, existence, permanent, abiding, eternal; also truthfulness in thought, word, and deed.

TWO FACES OF THE MASTER – The Inner Master, who is always with His students; and the outer Master, who writes, lectures, and teaches the outer studies to his followers.

U

UNION WITH GOD – Soul becomes a co-worker with God. Soul merges with the essence of God, not the Godhead Itself.

UNIVERSAL – That which is true or real within the entire body of the Creator, or soul's own existence; permanent, unchanging, random.

V

VANITY – I-ness, ego; one of the five deadly passions (lust, anger, greed, vanity, attachment); also one of the four divisions of mind, whose function is to separate self and self-interests from all else.

VEIL – Illusion or delusion; deception; unreality; the phenomenal universe. All that which is not eternal is not real and true. The veil of illusion conceals the vision of God from one's sight.

VIBRATION – Wave lengths in the specialized stream of Spirit; the whole life of any individual is one great wave length, as are music and electricity and every particle in the lower worlds.

VIRTUES – Antidotes to the five passions of the mind.

Passions	Virtues
Lust	Continence
Anger	Forgiveness
Greed	Contentment
Vanity	Humility
Attachment	Detachment

VOID, THE – A blank; the original place of all lower creations; emptiness in its own nature; being devoid of self-distinctiveness and independent from the elements which compose it; everything else is relative to it, but it has no relation to other things.

W

WORLDS OF THE SEEKER – The human consciousness, the psychic consciousness, and the spiritual consciousness; all three are lived in simultaneously and singularly, whether sleeping or awake.

Y

YOGA – Literally, union; esoterically, spiritual exercises, practice; meditation in the spiritual sense; any system which leads to or aims at the union of the soul with God.

Notes on Sources Quoted

Adi Granth (Granth Sahib): Sacred scripture of the Sikhs, compiled at the beginning of the 17th century by Guru Arjan Dev, the fifth Sikh guru. It includes original writings of the first five Sikh gurus and those attributed to many other spiritual teachers such as Kabir, Ramanand, Namdev, and Ravidas.

Aquinas, Thomas (1225-1274): Italian scholar and Dominican friar; saint of the Catholic Church. He taught theology in Paris, Rome, and Naples for twenty years; author of *Summa Contra Gentiles* and *Summa Theologica*.

Augustine (Aurelius Augustinus; *ca.* 354-430): Christian mystic and philosopher; saint of the Catholic Church; author of *The Confessions* and *On Grace and Free Will*.

Banyacya, Thomas (1909-): Hopi tribal and spiritual leader; Hopi elder since 1948; active spokesman of Native American wisdom and prophecies, urging world leaders to recognize and curtail the damage being done to the earth and to indigenous groups of people.

Besant, Annie (1847-1923): Author, speaker, social reformer; leader of Theosophical Society in early 20th century. Her work helped bring Eastern religious teachings to the West; author of *Seven Great Religions*.

Bible: Sacred scripture of Christianity. The first four books of The New Testament (*Matthew, Mark, Luke,* and *John*) are based on the oral teaching of Jesus. Written several decades after his crucifixion, they were modified by Church authorities over the centuries.

Buddha (Siddhartha Gautama; *ca.* 563-483 B.C.): Sage of Northern India who attained enlightenment and taught for four decades; his teachings are the basis of present-day Buddhism.

Bulleh Shah (*ca.* 1689-1753): Muslim mystic who taught in the Lahore District of the Punjab, openly expressing criticism of the Koran and Islamic ecclesiastical law.

Chuang Tzu (*ca.* 369-286 B.C.): Taoist philosopher and author. He inspired and wrote parts of the treatise, *Chuang Tzu,* which contains many of the same basic teachings of mysticism as the *Tao Te Ching,* but in a less political, more individualistic form.

Descartes, Rene (1596-1650): Philosopher, scientist, mathematician. He is recognized as the principal originator of the modern scientific method; author of *The Discourse on Method.*

Durckheim, Karlfried G. (1896-1988): German psychologist, author, philosopher; combined Zen Buddhism, modern psychology, and Christian mysticism to synthesize his understanding of the process of going within; author of many books on spirituality, including *The Call for the Master: The Meaning of Spiritual Guidance on the Way to the Self.*

Guru Amar Das (1479-1574): Third Sikh guru. He began the compilation of writings by various spiritual teachers which later were expanded by Guru Arjan Dev into the *Adi Granth.*

Guru Arjan Dev (1563-1606): Master of Light and Sound. Fifth Sikh guru. At the beginning of the 17th century he compiled the *Adi Granth* which includes his own compositions. Due to the growing strength of the Sikh movement, he was arrested by Mogul authorities and died in captivity; a major rift between Sikhs and Muslims followed.

Guru Nanak (*ca.* 1469-1539): Master of Light and Sound. First of the ten Sikh gurus in Northern India. His teachings, emphasizing love, devotion, and the inner spiritual journey, are included in the *Adi Granth* and formed the basis for the Sikh religion.

Hui-neng (638-713): Sixth Zen patriarch; uneducated woodcutter who studied under the Fifth Zen patriarch while working in the monastery kitchen. His deep penetration of the meaning of the Buddhist Sutras helped expand the Chinese Ch'an (Dhyana) School of Buddhism, forerunner of Zen Buddhism in Japan; author of the *Platform Sutra.*

Jagat Singh (1884-1951): Professor of Chemistry and Master of Light and Sound. He was the successor to Sawan Singh and spiritual Master at the Radha Soami Satsang at Beas in the Punjab region of India from 1948 to 1951; author of *The Science of the Soul.*

Jesus (*ca.* 4 B.C.-30 A.D.): Master of Light and Sound. Influenced by the Essenes and the Magi of Mesopotamia, he taught tolerance and love to Jews and Gentiles alike at a time of intense rivalry among religious as well as racial groups. His life and teaching were the basis for what later became Christianity.

Johnson, Julian (1873-1939): American minister, surgeon, aviator, and spiritual seeker. Late in life he became a close disciple of Sawan Singh, Master of Light and Sound, and remained with him in India from 1932 to 1939; author of *With a Great Master in India* and *The Path of the Masters.*

Jung, Carl (1875-1961): Swiss psychiatrist, philosopher, university professor. His approach emphasized the integration of our perception of the external world with our internal, mystical experience; author of many books on psychology, including *The Psychology of the Unconscious* and *Psychology and Religion.*

Kabir (*ca.* 1398-1518): Master of Light and Sound. Poet, weaver; well known Muslim saint of India. His writings initially were passed down orally and first appeared in 16th and 17th century manuscripts (the *Kabir Granthavali* and the *Adi Granth*).

Kirpal Singh (1894-1974): Disciple of Sawan Singh and founder of Ruhani Satsang in India; President of the United Nations World Fellowship of Religions for fourteen years; author of many books on Light and Sound, including *The Japji: The Message of Guru Nanak* and *The Crown of Life: A Study of Yoga.*

Koran: Sacred scripture of Islam; Muhammed's oral teachings delivered in Mecca and Medina over a period of twenty years, unified in written form within two decades after his death.

Krishnamurti, Jiddu (1895-1986): Mystic, author, lecturer. Born in India and trained by Theosophist leaders to be the next great World Teacher; he rejected the role in 1929 and became an independent lecturer throughout the world for the next fifty years.

Muhammed (570-632): Born in Mecca, he taught there and in Medina and was the founder of Islam. Sufism, which embraces the mystical aspects of the teaching, was formed by followers when they were forced to flee from Mecca.

Olsen, Gary (1948-): Master of Light and Sound. Lecturer and author of several books on Light and Sound, who began teaching in the United States in 1987; founder of MasterPath.

Rudhyar, Dane (1895-1985): Astrologer, composer, artist, philosopher. Contributed significantly to the early development of the New Age Movement, promoting the idea of world integration based on merging Eastern and Western concepts and attitudes; author of *Occult Preparations for the New Age* and *The Planetarization of Consciousness.*

Rumi (Maulana Rum; Jalal-ud-Din Rumi; 1207-1273): Master of Light and Sound; well-known Muslim saint and Sufi mystic of Persia; prolific writer and author of the world famous *Masnavi*; devoted disciple of Shamas-i-Tabriz.

Shamas-i-Tabriz (1206-1248): Master of Light and Sound; Muslim saint of Persia; Rumi's Master and the inspiration for Rumi's composition, *Divan-i-Shamas-i-Tabriz*.

Suzuki, D. T. (1869-1966): Author, lecturer, Buddhist scholar. Prolific writer in Japanese and English; played a major role in bringing Zen Buddhism to the West; author of many books, including *An Introduction to Zen Buddhism, Essays in Zen Buddhism,* and *Mysticism: Christian and Buddhist*.

Swami Ji Maharaj (Seth Shiv Dayal Singh; 1818-1878): Master of Light and Sound; founder of the Radha Soami spiritual path. After spending seventeen years in meditation, he began teaching in Northern India in 1861; author of *Sar Bachan*.

Tulsi Sahib (*ca.* 1764-1848): Master of Light and Sound; great poet-saint of India. Born into a royal family, he left home just before taking the throne and fled north to pursue his spiritual calling; author of *Ghat Ramayana* and *Ratan Sagar*.

INDEX

Abraham, 84, 87
Absence of desire, 76
Abu Bekr, 86
Accepting a Master, 131
Accident, 30
Act on own behalf,
    willingness to, 133
Act to know, 134
Adi Granth, 116
Adrenal gland, 47
Afterlife, 83, 97, 105
AIDS, 116
Alarm clock, divine, 143
Aloneness, 69, 97
Amar Das, 57, 147
Anarchy, 127
Andrews, Lynn, 101
Angels, 87
Anger, 18, 21, 25, 76
Animal kingdom, 18
Anti-materialism, 81
Aphrodite, 103
Aquarian Age, 131
Aquinas, Thomas 99
Archangels, 87, 89
Arjan Dev, 50
Armageddon, 111, 115-6
Ascetics, 76
Ashram, 64
Astral
    body, 9, 14-5, 18-9, 37-40, 48, 51,
        55-6, 76, 92, 95, 158
    plane, 15, 19, 35, 39, 67-8, 84, 98,
        105
    projection, 24, 35, 149
    worlds, 19, 23-4, 35, 156
Astrology, 9, 95-6, 98-100, 114
Athena, 103
Atlantis, 116
Atonement, 84
Attachment, 21, 76

Attention, 4-5, 10, 19-21, 27, 29, 36-8,
    44, 48, 61, 66, 96, 104, 128,
    133-7, 142-6, 157
Attitude, 23, 29, 33, 40, 58, 124, 128,
    131-2, 141, 144-8, 154, 157-8
Audible Life Stream, 8-9, 11-2, 40-4,
    48, 60, 62, 68-9, 74, 79, 83-4,
    92, 104, 117, 144, 146
Augustine, 38
Aura, 69, 96, 149
Authenticity
    of Master, 62, 64
    of Koran, 88
Avatars, 8, 108, 110, 120
Avoiding
    commitment, 125
    pain, 6, 20, 27, 42, 79, 129, 145
    present moment, 28
    rigidity, 157
Awakened state, 12, 147
Awakening of soul, 45, 48, 51, 57, 83,
    95-6, 101, 105-6, 118, 139, 143-7
Awareness, 3, 5, 9-11, 18, 21, 26, 37-
    40, 45-48, 58, 61, 66-9, 94, 99,
    100, 114-6, 119, 142-3, 150, 157
Aztecs, 110

Babylon, 109
Bagpipes, 10
Balance, 23-4, 29, 40, 42, 49, 63, 67,
    78-9, 101, 103, 110, 157
Banyacya, Thomas, 109
Baptism
    in the Holy Spirit, 84
    not necessary, 74
Battle, 4-5, 56, 70, 78, 84, 86, 111,
    115-6, 132
    of Armageddon, 111, 115-6
    of mind and soul, 70
Battlefield, 4-5, 56, 115
Beauty, 3-4, 20, 22, 31, 35, 46, 85, 94,